BUS OPERATOR CONDUCTOR

(NYCTA—MABSTOA)

BUS OPERATOR CONDUCTOR

(NYCTA—MABSTOA)

Edited by
Hy Hammer, Chief of
Examining Service Division
New York City Department
of Personnel (Ret.)

MACMILLAN • USA

Seventh Edition
Macmillan General Reference
A Simon & Schuster Macmillan Company
1633 Broadway
New York, NY 10019

Copyright © 1993, 1984, 1975, 1970, 1969, 1968, 1967 by Arco Publishing,
a division of Simon & Schuster, Inc.
All rights reserved
including the right of reproduction
in whole or in part in any form

An Arco Book

Library of Congress Cataloging-in-Publication Data

Bus operator, conductor: (NYCTA-MABSTOA)
   edited by Hy Hammer.—7th ed.
     p. cm.
  ISBN 0-671-87134-X
  1. Bus driving—Examinations, questions, etc. I. Hammer, Hy.
TL232.3B87   1993
629.28'333'076—dc20   93-6817
                                                      CIP

Manufactured in the United States of America

  7 8 9 10

TABLE OF CONTENTS

WHY AND HOW TO USE THIS BOOK 7

PART ONE
THE JOBS AND HOW TO GET THEM

THE KIND OF WORK YOU WILL BE DOING 11
    Bus Operator 12
    Conductor 13
QUALIFICATION AND TRAINING 15
    Bus Operator 15
    Conductor 17
COMMERCIAL LICENSING REQUIREMENTS 19
    Transporting Passengers 22
TEST-TAKING TECHNIQUES 25

PART TWO
SAMPLE EXAMS

FIRST SAMPLE EXAM, Bus Operator 33
SECOND SAMPLE EXAM, Bus Operator 53
THIRD SAMPLE EXAM, Conductor 75
FOURTH SAMPLE EXAM, Bus Operator/Conductor 97
FIFTH SAMPLE EXAM, Bus Operator/Conductor 117
CDL PERFORMANCE TESTS 135
    Pre-Trip Inspection Skills Test 135
    On-Road Skills Test 137
    Sample Evaluation Form 141

PART THREE
STUDY MATERIAL TO HELP YOU PASS YOUR TESTS

DEALING WITH EMERGENCIES 145
    Bus Operator 145
    Conductor 148
VEHICLE SAFETY 152
MUNICIPAL GEOGRAPHY 155

WHY AND HOW TO USE THIS BOOK

You have bought this book in hopes of getting a job as a bus operator or transit conductor. You have made a smart move. As cities strive to improve their air quality by cutting down on auto exhaust pollution, they are investing in their mass transit systems. Bus drivers and conductors are well paid and face a secure employment future. Furthermore, municipalities tend to offer attractive benefit packages and retirement systems that make your job even more valuable to you.

This book begins with descriptions of the work done by bus operators and conductors. It tells of job requirements, how to qualify, and what tests you will have to take. It also explains the training programs. You do not have to know how to drive a bus or how to be a conductor in order to be hired. Once you have proven that you can learn to do the job, the transit system will train you.

The first part of the book also goes into detail about the Commercial Drivers License (CDL) that bus operators must obtain. The CDL information comes from the manual published by the state of New York. However, the CDL rules are Federal rules, so the information applies equally in all fifty states.

The part ends with hints for earning a good score in multiple-choice examinations.

Part Two consists of sample examinations. The sample exams are compiled from actual bus operator and conductor exams used a number of years ago in New York city. If you are taking your exam in another city, you may not be able to answer some of the questions about where things are in New York, but these questions will give you a good idea of the kinds of questions that are asked. Your scores on the sample examinations are not important. These are not full-length previous exams; they are full-length exams made up out of previously used questions. The practice you get in answering these exams will help to prepare you for map reading, schedule interpretation, bulletin reading, and judgment questions you will find on the exam you will take.

The CDL questions are real, current CDL questions; the sample evaluation form is an actual form. After you have studied these, you will know exactly what to expect when you take your CDL exams.

The last part of the book offers you extra study material to help you as you prepare for your exam. The chapter concerning dealing with emergencies is important and useful for all transit system test-takers, for jobs above and below ground, in any locality. The vehicle safety chapter applies only to bus driver candidates, and the municipal geography chapter is limited to New York city applicants. Concentrate on the chapters that apply to you, then, if you have time, try the sample exams again.

PART ONE

The Jobs and How to Get Them

THE KIND OF WORK YOU WILL BE DOING

The increased use of privately owned automobiles in cities and the population shift to the suburbs, where most people drive their own cars, have created the twin problems of traffic congestion and air pollution. In fact, in urban areas the automobile is recognized as the single greatest cause of hazardous air pollution.

As part of the effort to reduce the number of cars congesting city streets, many cities are trying to improve local mass transit. Some cities are just beginning to develop subway systems. Where subways already exist, major efforts are underway to upgrade cars, tracks, safety, reliability, and general quality of service. Bus routes are the backbone of most urban and suburban transit. Besides modernizing the bus fleets, cities are taking innovative moves to lure greater ridership. Some now have commuter buses with reserved seats. In addition, express lanes reserved for buses on city streets and more convenient routes make bus transit quicker and more attractive to riders. Subways are the fastest means of urban transit, but buses offer the advantages of the passengers' being able to see where they are going and of minimal step-climbing. In fact, most transit buses are now "handicapped friendly."

Local transit systems relieve millions of Americans of the bother of fighting city traffic every day. These systems afford definite time schedules and definite routes to provide passengers with an alternative to automobile driving and even ownership.

Bus Operator

The workday for local bus drivers begins when they report to the terminal or garage to which they are assigned. Large cities have several garages while a small city may have only one. At the garage, drivers are given transfer and refund forms. Some are assigned buses and drive them to the start of their run. Others go to designated intersections and relieve drivers who are going off duty. Drivers inspect the inside and outside of the buses and check the tires, brakes, windshield wipers, and lights before starting their runs. Those who work for small bus companies also may check the water, oil, and fuel.

On most runs, drivers pick up and discharge passengers at locations marked with a bus stop sign. As passengers board the bus, drivers make sure the correct cash fare, token, or ticket is placed in the fare box. They also collect or issue transfers. Drivers often answer questions about schedules, routes, and transfer points, and sometimes call out the name of the street at each bus stop.

Bus drivers' days are run by the clock, as they must pay special attention to their complicated schedules. Although drivers may run late in heavier-than-average traffic, they avoid letting light traffic put them ahead of schedule, so that they do not miss passengers.

Bus drivers especially must be alert to the traffic around them. Since sudden stops or swerves will jar standing passengers, drivers try to anticipate traffic developments, not react to them.

At the end of the day, bus drivers turn in trip sheets which usually include a record of fares received, trips made and any significant delays in schedule. They also turn in a report on the mechanical condition of the bus that day. In case of an accident, drivers must make out a report describing exactly what happened before and after the event and obtain the names, addresses, and phone numbers of persons on the bus.

Most drivers have regularly scheduled runs. New drivers, however, often are placed on an "extra" list to substitute for regular drivers who are ill or on vacation. New drivers also may be assigned to make extra trips during morning and evening rush hours. They remain on the extra list until they have enough seniority to get a regular run. This may take several months or more than a year.

The different runs are assigned on the basis of length of service, or seniority. Therefore, as drivers develop seniority they can choose runs they prefer, such as those that lead to overtime, or that have little traffic.

Saturdays and Sundays are counted as regular workdays. Some drivers have to work evenings and after midnight. To accommodate the demands of commuter travel, many local bus drivers have to work "split shifts." For example, a driver might work from 6 a.m. to 10 a.m., go home, and then return to work from 3 p.m. to 7 p.m. Drivers may receive extra pay for split shifts.

Driving a bus is not physically strenuous, but bus drivers may suffer nervous strain from maneuvering a large vehicle through heavy traffic while dealing with passengers. However, local bus drivers enjoy steady year-round employment, and work without close supervision.

Conductor

Subway train conductors are immediately responsible for the safety, regularity, and proper care of trains in accordance with the rules, regulations, and special instructions governing the employees in operation.

Most conductors are assigned to trains. Their routine duties on the trains involve traffic control and crowd control. Conductors also give information about timetables, routes, and transfer points. They must be very knowledgeable about the subway system so as to be able to advise passengers about best routes, alternate routes, and connections. Conductors also must have thorough understanding of the equipment on the trains and how it works. They must know how the doors operate and how to solve door problems. Conductors work with motormen, track workers, and mechanics and maintainers to correct problems in the quickest possible time so as to keep the trains loading and unloading and moving on schedule.

As subway systems are upgraded and improved, there should be fewer emergencies. Even so, fire and smoke in subway tunnels constitute real dangers. It is the conductor's responsibility to safeguard passengers by assessing the extent of the smoke danger and by evacuating the passengers calmly, speedily, and safely according to the evacuation procedures of the transit system. The conductor must think quickly, act decisively, and do it the best way.

Most of the transit personnel in subway stations and on the platforms are Transit Police Officers or Property Protection Officers (Security Guards). However, some conductors are assigned to platform duty. These conductors must be extremely well informed not only about the entire subway system but about connecting buses as well. They must also be experts in crowd control and in moving large groups of people safely. They must also be aware of the location of backup personnel and facilities and know how to size up and deal with emergencies that may occur.

There was a time when subway conductors also saw lots of duty in the train yards. Today, most switches are automatic or are tower operated, so conductors are seldom used in the yards. The conductors who do choose yard duty—a choice job—must understand the operation of switches and the special safety requirements that apply in the yards.

QUALIFICATION AND TRAINING

There are no education requirements for either the bus operator or conductor position; however, applicants must pass a written examination that determines whether they are capable of learning the duties of the job and performing well once assigned. In addition, all applicants must take a thorough medical examination. Operating personnel are entrusted with the safety of the traveling public. They must have good eyesight and hearing, agility, stamina, and reliable health so as to perform all of their duties on a sustained basis. Bus operators and conductors are subject to random drug testing. There is no physical performance test for either position.

Bus Operator

Candidates for bus operator must score over 70% on a multiple-choice examination. Subjects of the written test are: rules of the road and safe driving; driving regulations; courtesy to passengers; safety procedures; procedures in case of accidents, injury, or crimes; ability to read bulletins, route maps, and schedules; points of interest in the city. Applicants with the highest scores are placed at the top of the eligible list. Hiring is made from the top of the list, so it is to your advantage to study for the written test and to earn the highest possible score.

Besides passing the written test and the medical examination, bus operator candidates must have a valid driver's license clear of serious moving violations, license suspensions, or accidents. By the time of hiring, bus operator applicants must have obtained a Class B learner's permit.

A relaxed personality, while not a requirement for hiring, is important since drivers face many minor irritations each day due to traffic congestion, bad weather, and the many different, and sometimes difficult, personalities they must deal with.

Once hired, new bus operators undergo an intensive 30-day training program. During this training, new hires learn to drive transit buses in preparation for the Class B operator's license. Included in the bus operation training is defensive driving instruction. Because a bus driver is seated above other traffic, defensive driving—seeing and avoiding possible traffic dangers ahead of time—is a potential life saver. Defensive driving is stressed because of its value to the driver and the transit system and because it is required by law.

The training sessions include both classroom and "behind-the-wheel" instruction. In the classroom, trainees learn company rules, safety regulations, and safe driving practices. They also learn how to keep records and how to deal tactfully and courteously with passengers. New drivers learn passenger handling techniques, safety procedures, routes, and customer relations. They also learn how to use the communications system with which they have been provided. New York City Transit Authority buses were equipped with a sophisticated new radio network in 1991. The system includes a panic button for use in major emergencies; provision to request priority voice communication in urgent situations; and regular voice communication channels as well. Other bus companies may have other systems. You will be trained to use whatever system you carry.

The actual driver training includes a week of training in bus handling at a remote, uncluttered location; a week of driving an empty bus under increasingly difficult conditions; and two weeks of supervised passenger-carrying in traffic. Driver training also includes instruction in the thorough morning check of a transit bus; walk-around check to be done by a driver picking up a bus on relief; and preparation of the defect card at the end of the day.

All of this driver training concludes with the state test for a Class B operator's license with passenger endorsement. All new transit employees serve a probationary period, usually one year, during which they must prove their competence. During the probationary period a new employee may be terminated for reasonable cause without right of appeal. After probation, the permanent employee is subject to union protection. In addition to maintaining the work and conduct standards of the department, the driver must maintain the highest driving standards. The state requires an annual defensive driving review and both written and road tests every other year. The New York City Transit Authority and many other municipal systems perform written and road retests every year. Bus operators must maintain good driving records in their personal lives as well as in the bus driver's seat. They are not permitted to accumulate "points" during off-duty automobile driving. And, of course, they must submit to and pass random drug testing whenever called.

Conductor

Candidates for the conductor position must also score 70% or better on a multiple-choice examination. The conductor examination stresses: dealing with the public and handling municipal property; reading and interpreting instructions, rules and regulations, transit bulletins and transit schedules; interpreting route maps and selecting proper transfer points, best routes and best alternate routes; interpreting timetables and work programs; and location of major points of interest and significant landmarks in the city. The examination also looks for signs of good judgment and common sense. As with the bus operator list, the eligible list is formed with the names of top scorers at the top, and hiring is done from the top of the list. Qualified veterans may be able to boost passing scores by adding additional points. You can only add veteran's points to a score that is a passing score without them. If you think that you qualify, inquire in your own city. Use of veteran's credits varies by city and state.

Conductor candidates must pass medical examination and random drug testing on request, but do not need to meet any driving requirements.

Once hired, conductors are trained in crowd control and traffic control. They receive detailed instruction in the operation of equipment on subway trains—public address systems, hand held radios, and especially the doors. Problem analysis and problem solution both enter into the education process. An important subject of repeated drills is evacuation procedure under varying emergency conditions—smoke, fire, power outage. Conductors learn to size up emergencies and to choose the proper evacuation procedures for each. They also get intensive practice with interpreting timetables and work programs. And, of course, they learn to use maps and learn the lines, routes, and stops. Newly hired conductors also learn to fill out the required reports of daily occurrences and emergencies.

As with bus operators, conductors serve a probationary period after which they become permanent employees of the system.

COMMERCIAL LICENSING REQUIREMENTS

Every bus operator must possess a Class B commercial driver's license with a passenger endorsement. By the time you are assigned to a route, you too must have this license. The transit authority has an intensive, effective training program in which it teaches new hires to drive transit buses safely and according to the law. You do not need to have a class B license in order to be hired, but you do need to have obtained a commercial driver's learner's permit. If you are not already a licensed driver, you must first learn to drive a car and obtain a driver's license. Obviously, you will need a few years' experience driving a passenger car before you can even think of handling a large, bulky bus. When you are ready to move up to buses, you pick up forms and information at your Motor Vehicles Bureau. The state of New York puts out a 150-page book entitled *Commercial Driver's Manual, Class A, B & C Licenses*. This book is distributed free of charge at Motor Vehicles offices. It contains all the information you need to pass the written tests. You must pass the written tests and meet all other prerequisite requirements in order to get the learner's permit.

To get a CDL, you must pass knowledge (written) tests and a skills (road) test to ensure that you have the minimum knowledge and skill required to drive a commercial motor vehicle.

You will have to pass one or more knowledge tests, depending on the class of license and the endorsements you need. Each test will be scored separately. The passing score is 80% for all commercial knowledge tests.

The CDL knowledge tests that apply to bus drivers include:

BASIC TESTS

- **General Knowledge** for all applicants.
- **Air Brakes** to operate a CMV with air brakes.

ENDORSEMENT TESTS

• **Passenger transport** for all bus drivers (including drivers who carry 15 or more passengers and those who are included under Article 19-A). Once you pass the knowledge tests, you can then take the CDL skills test which is divided into 3 parts. These parts are:

1) Pre-Trip Inspection

You must do a pre-trip inspection of your vehicle to make sure it is safe to drive. You must explain to the examiner what you are inspecting and why. The examiner will note each item that you correctly inspected. If the vehicle fails the pre-trip inspection because it is unsafe, your test will not be completed, and you will have to schedule a new test with a safe vehicle.

2) Basic Control Skills

You must complete several exercises including parallel parking, straight line backing, and forward stopping to evaluate your basic skills in controlling the vehicle. The examiner will explain how each exercise is to be done. You will be scored on how well you perform the exercises.

3) Road Test

You must drive over a route specified by the examiner, and show you can drive safely in on-the-road situations. The route may include left and right turns, intersections, railway crossings, curves, up and down grades, rural or suburban roads, urban multi-lane streets, and expressway driving.

You will drive over the test route following instructions given by the examiner. The examiner will score turns, merging into traffic, lane changes, and speed control at specific places along the route. The examiner will also score whether you correctly do tasks such as signaling, searching for hazards, and lane positioning. You will be told whether or not you passed at the end of the road test. There is no waiting period.

You will automatically fail the test if you have an accident, commit a serious traffic violation, or take a dangerous action during the road test.

You must take the skills test in a vehicle representative of those that may be driven with the license class you've applied for. After about five weeks of investment in your training, the transit authority will arrange for the appropriate bus for you to take your test on.

Passenger Transport (Bus) Operation

There is no separate commercial license class for buses. Instead, a passenger transport endorsement is required. If you want to drive a bus, you must pass the general knowledge test, the passenger transport endorsement test, and the skills test in a bus representative of Class B or C. Passing the skills test in a bus will also qualify you to drive trucks in the same class, although endorsements may be necessary depending on the type of truck or its use. However, a Class B or C license holder cannot drive a bus of any weight without a passenger endorsement.

Passenger endorsement may be restricted by the GVWR of the vehicle and/or by a passenger seating capacity of less than fifteen.

Air Brakes Restriction

To drive a commercial vehicle with air brakes, you must also pass an air brakes knowledge test and the skills test in a vehicle with air brakes. Otherwise, your license will be issued with a "Not Valid for Air Brakes" restriction. Most transit buses, including all those in use in New York City, have air brakes.

Commercial Driver License Requirements

To get a Class B learner's permit you must already have a valid NYS driver's license. In addition, you must:

- Be at least 18 years of age.
- Complete an application (MV-44).
- Provide proof of identity, residency, date of birth, and your social security number.
- Pay the application/testing fee.
- Pass the vision test.
- Pass the general knowledge test and any necessary supplemental tests.
- Pay the skills test fee, the permit/license fee, and the photo fee.

The learner's permit must be for the proper class and include any endorsements required for driving the practice vehicle. The permit holder must be accompanied at all times by a driver holding a commercial driver's license with the proper class and any required endorsements. The permit and the supervising driver's license must not have any restrictions which would prohibit driving the practice vehicle.

To get a commercial driver's license, you must:

- Pass the skills test in a representative vehicle.
- Certify:
  (1) that you are not disqualified from driving and your driver's license or driving privilege is not suspended, revoked, or canceled in any jurisdiction.
  (2) that you do not have more than one driver's license.
  (3) that the vehicle used for skills testing is representative of the type of vehicle you operate or expect to operate.
  (4) whether or not you are qualified under federal regulations for interstate (state to state) operation.
- Turn in all driver's licenses you have.

Under New York State law, any person who operates a motor vehicle in New York is deemed to have given consent to a chemical test of one or more of the following: breath, blood, urine, or saliva for the purpose of determining the alcoholic and/or drug content of the blood.

A driver holding a CDL issued by another jurisdiction who moves to New York must apply for a New York CDL within 30 days after establishing residency.

All bus drivers in New York State must have CDLs and employers must determine that the drivers they hire are qualified to drive buses. Furthermore, Article 19-A of the NYS Vehicle and Traffic Law sets standards for bus drivers. Under this law, **employers of BUS DRIVERS must**:

- Conduct background investigations of a new driver's employment history for the past 3 years.
- Obtain driving records from all jurisdictions where the driver worked, lived, or had a driver's license or learner's permit in the past 3 years.
- Tell drivers about the provisions of Article 19-A.
- Require that drivers take an initial physical examination and then follow-up exams **every two years**.
- Annually review the driving record of each driver to determine if he/she meets the minimum requirements to drive a bus.
- Annually observe each driver's defensive driving performance while operating a bus carrying passengers.
- Give each driver a behind-the-wheel driving test **every two years**. The New York City Transit Authority repeats the driving test every year.
- Give each driver a written or oral examination **every two years** to test his/her knowledge of the rules of the road, defensive driving practices and laws regulating bus driving in New York State. The New York City Transit Authority exceeds the requirement by repeating the knowledge test every year.
- Subject a driver who fails to provide notification of convictions to a five working-day suspension or a suspension equivalent to the number of working days a driver was not in compliance with reporting requirements, whichever is longer.

If a bus driver fails to meet any of the 19-A requirements, the employer must not allow him/her to operate a bus until the requirements are met.

The Department of Motor Vehicles also disqualifies drivers based on their driving record and criminal history.

Under the federal Commercial Motor Vehicle Safety Act of 1986 (CMVSA/86), all commercial drivers must:

- **Have only one driver's license.** If you break this law, you may be fined up to $5,000 or put in jail. **Keep your home state license and immediately return any other licenses to the state where they were issued.**
- **Notify their employer within 30 days of a conviction for any traffic violation** (except parking). This is true no matter where or what type of vehicle you were driving. **Note: Article 19-A bus drivers must report convictions to their employer within five working days from the date of conviction.**
- **If licensed in New York, notify the New York State Department of Motor Vehicles within 30 days of an out-of-state conviction for any traffic violation** (except parking). This is true no matter what type of vehicle you were driving.
- **Notify their employer** by the end of the next business day **if their license is suspended, revoked, canceled, or if they are disqualified** from driving. **Your employer must not let you drive a CMV** if you have more than one license, if your CDL is suspended, revoked, or canceled, or you are disqualified from driving. You may be fined up to $5,000 or face jail for breaking this law.
- **When applying for a commercial driving job, give the employer information** on all driving jobs held for the past 10 years.

Transporting Passengers

Bus drivers must have a commercial driver's license if they drive a vehicle designed to carry 15 or more passengers (excluding the driver) **OR** a vehicle defined as a bus under Article 19-A Section 509(a) of the Vehicle and Traffic Law. However, you are not considered a bus driver if you only carry family members for nonbusiness purposes.

Bus drivers must have a passenger endorsement on their commercial driver's license. To get the endorsement you must pass a written test. If your bus has air brakes, you must also pass a written test on air brakes. You must also pass the performance tests required for the class of vehicle you drive. Here is information you must know to drive a bus safely.

Before driving your bus, make sure it is safe. During the pre-trip inspection, check defects reported by previous drivers. Only if defects reported earlier have been fixed, should you sign the previous driver's report. This is your certification that the defects reported earlier have been fixed.

Make sure these things are in good working order before driving:

- Service brakes
- Parking brake
- Steering mechanism
- Lights and reflectors
- Tires (front wheels must not have recapped or regrooved tires)
- Horn
- Windshield wipers
- Rear-vision mirrors
- Wheels and rims

As you check the outside of the bus, close any open emergency exits. Also close any open access panels before driving.

People sometimes damage unattended buses. Always check the interior of the bus before driving to ensure rider safety. Aisles and stairwells must always be clear. The following parts of your bus must be in safe working condition:

- Each handhold and railing
- Floor covering
- Signaling devices
- Emergency exit handles

The seats must be safe for riders. All seats must be securely fastened to the bus.

Never drive with an open emergency exit door or window. The "Emergency Exit" sign on an emergency door must be clearly visible. If there is a red emergency door light, it must work. Turn it on at night or any other time you use your outside lights.

You may lock some emergency roof hatches in a partly open position for fresh air. Do not leave them open as a regular practice. Keep in mind the bus's higher clearance while driving with them open.

Make sure your bus has the fire extinguisher and emergency reflectors required by law. The bus must also have spare electrical fuses unless equipped with circuit breakers.

The driver's seat should have a seat belt. Always use it for safety.

Do not allow riders to leave carry-on baggage in a doorway or aisle. There should be nothing in the aisle that might trip other riders. Secure baggage and freight in ways that avoid damage and:

- allow the driver to move freely and easily.
- allow riders to exit by any window or door in an emergency.
- protect riders from injury if carry-ons fall or shift.

No rider may stand forward of the rear of the driver's seat. Buses designed to allow standing must have a 2-inch line on the floor or some other means of showing riders where they cannot stand. This is called the standee line. All standing riders must stay behind it.

Don't talk with riders or engage in any other distracting activity while driving.

While driving, scan the interior of your bus as well as the road ahead, to the sides, and to the rear. You may have to remind riders about rules or to keep arms and heads inside the bus.

Do not tow or push a disabled bus with riders aboard either vehicle unless getting off would be unsafe. Only tow or push the bus to the nearest safe spot to discharge passengers. Follow your employer's guidelines on towing or pushing disabled buses.

Urban mass transit coaches may have a brake and accelerator interlock system. The interlock applies the brakes and holds the throttle in idle position when the rear door is open. The interlock releases when you close the rear door. Do not use this safety feature in place of the parking brake.

Riders can stumble when getting on or off and when the bus starts or stops. Caution riders to watch their step when leaving the bus. Wait for them to sit down or brace themselves before starting. Starting and stopping should be as smooth as possible to avoid rider injury.

Occasionally, you may have a drunk or disruptive rider. You must ensure this rider's safety as well as that of others. Don't discharge such riders where it would be unsafe for them. It may be safer at the next scheduled stop or a well lighted area where there are other people. Many carriers have guidelines for handling disruptive riders.

Bus crashes often happen at intersections. Use caution, even if a signal or stop sign controls other traffic. School and mass transit buses sometimes scrape off mirrors or hit passing vehicles when pulling out from a bus stop. Remember the clearance your bus needs and watch for poles and tree limbs at stops. Know the size of the gap your bus needs to accelerate and merge with traffic. Wait for the gap to open before leaving the stop. Never assume other drivers will brake to give you room when you signal or start to pull out.

Crashes on curves kill people and destroy buses. They result from excessive speed, often when rain or snow has made the road slippery. Every banked curve has a safe "design speed." In good weather, the posted speed is safe for cars, but it may be too high for many buses. With good traction, the bus may roll over; with poor traction, it might slide off the curve. **Reduce speed for curves!** If your bus leans toward the outside on a banked curve, you are driving too fast.

Stop your bus between 15 and 50 feet before railroad crossings. Listen and look in both directions for trains. You should open your forward door if it improves your ability to see or hear an approaching train. Before crossing after a train has passed, make sure there isn't another train coming in the other direction on other tracks. If your bus has a manual transmission, don't change gears while crossing the tracks.

You do not have to stop, but must slow down and carefully check for other vehicles:

- at street car crossings.
- at railroad tracks used only for industrial switching within a business district.
- where a policeman or flagman is directing traffic.
- if a traffic signal shows green.
- at crossings marked "exempt crossing."

Stop at drawbridges that do not have a signal light or traffic control attendant. Stop at least 50 feet before the draw of the bridge. Look to make sure the draw is completely closed before crossing. You do not need to stop, but must slow down and make sure it's safe, when:

- there is a traffic light showing green.
- the bridge has an attendant or traffic officer who controls traffic whenever the bridge opens.

Inspect your bus at the end of each shift. You must complete a written inspection report for each bus driven. The report must specify each bus and list any defect that would affect safety or result in a breakdown. If there are no defects, the report should say so.

Riders sometimes damage safety related parts such as hand-holds, seats, emergency exits, and windows. If you report this damage at the end of a shift, mechanics can make repairs before the bus goes out again. Mass transit drivers should also make sure passenger signaling devices and brake-door interlocks work properly.

TEST-TAKING TECHNIQUES

Many factors enter into a test score. The most important factor should be ability to answer the questions correctly. Ability to answer exam questions should be closely related to ability to learn and to perform the duties of the job. Assuming that you have this ability, it is important to know what to expect on the exam and be familiar with techniques of effective test-taking. This will ease the anxiety which might interfere with concentration and should increase speed and efficiency, enabling you to answer more questions and thereby raise your score.

On Examination Day

On the examination day assigned to you, allow the test itself to be the main attraction of the day. Do not squeeze it in between other activities. Arrive rested, relaxed, and on time. In fact, plan to arrive a little bit early. Leave plenty of time for traffic tie-ups or other complications which might upset you and interfere with your test performance. Remember to bring a few sharpened #2 pencils with clean erasers, positive identification with your picture or at least your signature, and whatever admission ticket or other papers you were instructed to bring. You will not be admitted to the exam if you have forgotten the required documents.

In the test room the examiner will hand out forms for you to fill out. He or she will give you instructions that you must follow in taking the examination. The examiner may distribute pencils for marking the answer sheet and will tell you how to fill in the grids on the forms. Time limits and timing signals will be explained. If you do not understand any of the examiner's instructions, ask questions. Make sure that you know exactly what to do.

At the examination, you must follow instructions exactly. Fill in the grids on the forms carefully and accurately. Filling in the wrong grid may lead to loss of veterans' credits to which you may be entitled or to an incorrect address for your test results. Do not begin until you are told to begin. Stop as soon as the examiner tells you to stop. Do not turn any pages until you are told to. If your exam is in parts, do not go back to any parts you have already completed. Any infraction of the rules is considered cheating. If you cheat, your test paper will not be scored, and you will not be eligible for appointment.

Using the Answer Sheet

Your exam will probably be machine scored. You cannot give any explanations to the machine, so you must fill out the answer sheet clearly and correctly.

1. Blacken your answer space completely. ● is the only correct way to mark the answer sheet. ◐, ⊗, ⊘, and ∅ are all unacceptable. The machine might not read them at all.
2. Mark only one answer for each question. If you mark more than one answer you will be considered wrong even if one of the answers is correct.

3. If you change your mind, you must erase your mark. Attempting to cross out an incorrect answer like this ✖ will not work. You must erase any incorrect answer completely. An incomplete erasure might be read as a second answer.
4. All of your answers should be in the form of blackened spaces. The machine cannot read English. Do not write any notes in the margins.
5. MOST IMPORTANT: Answer each question in the right place. Question 1 must be answered in space 1; question 23 in space 23. If you should skip an answer space and mark a series of answers in the wrong places, you must erase all those answers and do the questions over, marking your answers in the proper places. You cannot afford to use the limited time in this way. Therefore, as you answer *each* question, look at its number and check that you are marking your answer in the space with the same number.

What About Guessing?

You may be wondering whether or not it is wise to guess when you are not sure of an answer. Scoring of almost all civil service exams is on the basis of "rights only." The more questions you answer correctly, the higher your score. On these exams there is no penalty for a wrong answer. If you guess incorrectly, you have nothing to lose; but if you do not mark an answer, you cannot get a point. Ask to be sure about your exam. If there is no penalty for guessing incorrectly, by all means guess.

Obviously, an educated guess is worth more than a wild guess. When you are not certain of an answer, read the question and the answer choices very carefully. Eliminate those choices which are certainly wrong. Then try to reason from the remaining choices. Narrow the field as much as you can, then guess from among those choices which are left. The odds of guessing right improve as the number of choices from which you guess gets smaller.

Since you cannot score a point without marking an answer and since a wrong answer does not count against you, it is foolish to leave any blank spaces. Keep track of time. When you notice that time is about to run out, use the last few seconds to complete the exam part, even without reading the questions. Just choose a letter and mark all the remaining blanks with the same answer. According to the law of averages, you should get some portion of those answers right. If yours is the unusual exam which deducts points for wrong answers, do not fill in leftover spaces at time-up.

How Is the Exam Scored?

When the exam is over, the examiner will collect test booklets and answer sheets. The answer sheets will be sent to a central test center where a machine will scan your answers and mark them right or wrong. Then your raw score will be calculated. Your raw score is the number of questions you answered correctly.

This is not your final score. Raw scores are converted by formula to scaled scores, usually on a scale of 1 to 100.

In some locations, the written exam is competitive and candidates with the highest scores have the best chance of being hired. In other places, the written exam is qualifying. This means that the applicant qualifies for further consideration just by passing the written exam. Where the written exam is qualifying, appointment is usually based on a competitive physical performance exam. Other localities combine scores on written and performance exams into a single competitive score.

Except where appointment is made by lottery from among all passing applicants, appointment is made first from among the top scorers. If you are entitled to veterans' service points, these are added to the score you earned. Veterans' points are added only to passing scores. A failing score cannot be brought to passing level by veterans' points, but if you pass, veterans' points can help you get the job.

Recap of the Rules

1. Read every word of the instructions. Read every word of every question. Little words like *not*, *all*, or *except* may make a big difference in determining the correct answer.
2. Read all the answer choices before you mark your answer. It is statistically true that most errors are made when the correct answer is the last choice. Too many people mark the first answer that seems correct without reading through all the choices to find out which answer is best.
3. Mark your answers by completely blackening the answer space of your choice.
4. Mark only **one** answer for each question, even if you think that more than one answer is correct. You must choose only one. If you mark more than one answer, the scoring machine will consider you wrong.
5. If you change your mind, erase completely. Leave no doubt as to which answer you mean.
6. If you figure math in the margins of the test booklet, don't forget to mark the answer on the answer sheet. Only the answer sheet is scored. A correct answer in the margin of the test booklet does not count.
7. Check often to be sure that the question number matches the answer space, this will ensure that you have not skipped a space by mistake.
8. Guess as intelligently as you can, but be sure to answer all the questions.
9. Stay alert. Be careful not to mark a wrong answer from lack of concentration.
10. Do not panic. The person beside you who is way ahead of you may be making lots of mistakes. Just do your best.
11. Check and recheck if time permits. If you finish early, check to be sure that each question is answered in the right space and that there is only one answer for each question. Return to the difficult questions and rethink them.

Good Luck!

PART TWO

Sample Exams

FIRST SAMPLE EXAM

Bus Operator

DIRECTIONS: Each question has four suggested answers lettered A, B, C, and D. Decide which one is the best answer and on the sample answer sheet find the question number which corresponds to the answer that you have selected. Darken the area with a soft pencil.

The time allowed for the entire examination is 3 hours.

Questions 1-3 are based on the schedule for running time shown below. Running time is the scheduled time for a bus to travel from one stop to the next. The arrow indicates the direction in which the bus travels. For example, the running time from Main St. to School St., eastbound, is 5 minutes during the hours from 10:00 P.M. to 6:00 A.M., and 9 minutes from 6:00 A.M. to 10:00 P.M. If you want to know when a bus that leaves School Street at 11:00 P.M. should arrive at Pearl Street, you should add the 14 minutes running time to 11:00 P.M. to obtain 11:14 P.M.

RUNNING TIME

Bus Stop	10:00 P.M. to 6:00 A.M.		6:00 A.M. to 10:00 P.M.	
	Eastbound	Westbound	Eastbound	Westbound
Main St. to School St.	5	6 ↑	9	11 ↑
to Bank St.	4	5	7	8
to Market St.	5	6	10	12
to Pearl St.	5	6	9	11
to State St.	4 ↓	5	7 ↓	8
Totals	23	28	42	50

1. An eastbound bus leaves School St. at 1:30 P.M. At what time will it arrive at Market St.?

    (A) 1:30 P.M.
    (B) 1:41 P.M.
    (C) 1:47 P.M.
    (D) 1:50 P.M.

2. If a passenger boarding a westbound bus at State St. wishes to be at Bank St. by 3:00 P.M. the last bus he should take is one that leaves no later than

    (A) 2:21 P.M.
    (B) 2:29 P.M.
    (C) 2:34 P.M.
    (D) 2:43 P.M.

3. A westbound bus leaves Pearl Street at 11 P.M. but has an 18 minute delay because of a sick passenger at Market Street. The bus is delayed for another 4 minutes due to a broken traffic light at School Street. What time will the bus arrive at Main Street?

    (A) 11:45 P.M.   (B) 11:50 P.M.   (C) 12:07 A.M.   (D) 12:15 A.M.

4. To help prevent passenger accidents inside a bus, which of the following starting and stopping procedures should a bus operator follow?

    (A) gradual acceleration when starting and gradual slowing down when stopping
    (B) rapid acceleration when starting and rapid braking when stopping
    (C) gradual acceleration when starting and rapid braking when stopping
    (D) rapid acceleration when starting and gradual slowing down when stopping

5. When a bus operator is driving a bus, a flashing yellow light at an intersection means that he should

    (A) stop
    (B) stop, then proceed slowly
    (C) proceed with caution
    (D) maintain his speed through the intersection

Questions 6 through 8 are based on the schedule for Headway shown below. Headway is the scheduled time between one bus and the next bus, and this varies according to the time of day. For example, from 12 noon to 4 P.M., the time between buses is 10 minutes, and from 5:00 A.M. to 9:00 A.M. it is 5 minutes.

HEADWAY

	Minutes
5:00 A.M. to 9:00 A.M.	5
9:00 A.M. to 12:00 Noon	8
12:00 Noon to 4:00 P.M.	10
4:00 P.M. to 7:00 P.M.	5
7:00 P.M. to 11:00 P.M.	15
11:00 P.M. to 5:00 A.M.	30

6. At 7:00 A.M. a man just misses a bus. About how many minutes will he have to wait for the next bus?

   (A) 5 (B) 8 (C) 9 (D) 11

7. At 8:33 P.M. a woman arrives at a bus stop. The last bus left her stop on schedule 3 minutes ago. The next scheduled bus has been cancelled due to faulty equipment. The bus following the cancelled bus is running three minutes late because of heavy traffic. At what time should another bus arrive at the woman's stop?

   (A) 8:40 A.M. (B) 8:57 P.M. (C) 9:03 P.M. (D) 9:06 P.M.

8. What is the difference between the headway times at 11:50 A.M. and 11:20 P.M.?

   (A) 15 minutes (B) 20 minutes (C) 22 minutes (D) 25 minutes

9. In heavy traffic, which of the following turn situations is potentially most hazardous?

   (A) right turn from one two-way street onto another two-way street
   (B) left turn from a one-way street onto a two-way street
   (C) right turn from a two-way street onto a one-way street
   (D) left turn from one two-way street onto another two-way street

10. As you approach an intersection in your bus, you note that the traffic light is red and you hear the wailing noise of an ambulance siren. A police officer at the intersection motions for you to go through the light. Under the circumstances, you should

    (A) stop until you can determine the location of the ambulance
    (B) stop until the light turns green, then proceed
    (C) proceed to the middle of the intersection and stop so that you can better determine the location of the ambulance
    (D) proceed through the intersection

11. Which of the following actions should a bus operator take if he notices a boy climbing on the back of his bus?

    (A) Reduce speed and continue on his route.
    (B) Make sudden stops and starts to shake the boy off.
    (C) Stop the bus, inform his passengers why he is stopping, and then order the boy off the bus.
    (D) Ignore the boy and continue his trip at a normal speed.

Questions 12 through 15 are based on the schedule printed below. Running time is the scheduled time for a bus to travel from one stop to the next. The arrow indicates the direction in which the bus travels. For example, the running time from the Railroad Station to Main & Oak is 5 minutes. Lay-over time is the time spent at the terminal before leaving on the next trip.

Bus Stop	Southbound Running Time (Minutes)	Northbound Running Time (Minutes)
Railroad Station	(leaves)	5
Main & Oak	5	4
Main & Elm	4	6
Main & Ash	6	3
Main & Pine	3	5
Main & Birch	5	4
Farmer's Market	4	8
Plum & State	8	7
Apple & State	7	7
Pear & State	7	6
Peach & State	6	5
Court House	5	(leaves)

Note: Lay-over time at each of the terminals, "Railroad Station Terminal" and "Court House Terminal," is 5 minutes.

12. What is the running time in minutes from Peach and State northbound to Main & Ash?

    (A) 37   (B) 40   (C) 42   (D) 45

13. If a bus leaves the Railroad Station at 8:10 A.M., at what time should it arrive at the Court House?

    (A) 9:05 A.M.   (B) 9:08 A.M.   (C) 9:10 A.M.   (D) 9:12 A.M.

14. If a bus leaves the Court House at 9:05 A.M., at what time should it arrive at Farmer's Market?

    (A) 9:30 A.M.   (B) 9:35 A.M.   (C) 9:38 A.M.   (D) 9:43 A.M.

15. How much time will it take a bus leaving Main and Pine southbound to arrive back at Main and Pine on the return trip?

    (A) 1 hour, 17 minutes
    (B) 1 hour, 19 minutes
    (C) 1 hour, 29 minutes
    (D) 1 hour, 33 minutes

Answer questions 16 through 20 solely on the basis of the "Bus Operator's Daily Trip Sheet" shown below. At each terminal, at the end of a trip, the operator takes the readings on the cash counter and the token counter which are part of the fare box, and meters them on the "Bus Operator's Daily Trip Sheet." The part of the "Bus Operator's Daily Trip Sheet" shown below is a record of the fare box readings for a specific working day for Bus Operator Birch. Note that a trip covers the distance from one terminal to the other. When Operator Birch left the Rowland Street terminal for the first trip of his working day, the cash counter registered $225.00 from a previous operator's run and the token counter registered 113 tokens. Birch left Rowland Terminal at 12:51 P.M. and completed his first trip over the route and arrived at the Tully Street Terminal at 1:28 P.M. Assume that at each terminal arriving and leaving times are identical. For the remainder of his working day, he rode back and forth along his route, arriving at the Rowland and Tully terminals at the times indicated on the "Bus Operator's Daily Trip Sheet." His farebox readings were taken and entered on the trip sheet shown below immediately upon arrival at the terminals. When answering the questions, assume the fare is $1.00 and that all passengers are required to pay the full fare. Also assume that the tokens collected are worth $1.00 each.

BUS OPERATOR'S DAILY TRIP SHEET

POINT LEAVING FROM	TIME	FAREBOX READINGS AT THE END OF EACH TRIP	
		CASH	TOKENS
ROWLAND ST. TERMINAL	12:51 PM	225.00	113
TULLY ST. TERMINAL	1:28 PM	252.00	117
ROWLAND ST. TERMINAL	2:08 PM	270.00	122
TULLY ST. TERMINAL	2:45 PM	297.00	131
ROWLAND ST. TERMINAL	3:25 PM	330.00	133
TULLY ST. TERMINAL	4:04 PM	368.00	144
ROWLAND ST. TERMINAL	4:38 PM	404.00	147
TULLY ST. TERMINAL	5:18 PM	410.00	148

16. How much cash was collected between 1:28 P.M. and 3:25 P.M.?

    (A) $35.00   (B) $76.50   (C) $78.00   (D) $109.00

17. How many tokens were collected between 2:45 P.M. and 4:38 P.M.?

    (A) 16   (B) 17   (C) 25   (D) 147

18. What is the value of the tokens collected from 12:51 P.M. to 5:18 P.M.?

    (A) $32.40   (B) $35.00   (C) $30.00   (D) $41.00

19. How many passengers got on the bus between 2:08 P.M. and 4:04 P.M.?

    (A) 133   (B) 120   (C) 147   (D) 121

20. What was the total number of passengers carried during the entire run from 12:51 P.M. to 5:18 P.M.?

    (A) 245   (B) 269   (C) 220   (D) 251

38 / Bus Operator

Answer questions 21 through 27 solely on the basis of the description of the accident and the "Accident Report" shown below. The "Accident Report" contains 38 numbered spaces. Read the description and look at the "Accident Report" before answering the questions.

Description of accident: At 1:15 P.M., on July 20, 1988, an auto with license plate #51 VOM-NY, driven by Martha Ryan, license number R21692-33739-295897-41, and owned by George Ryan, traveling east on Fulton Street, crashed into the right front wheel of a moving Flexible bus, T.A. Vehicle No. 7026, license plate no. 10346-K, at the intersection of Jay Street and Fulton Street. The bus was covering Run 12 on Route B67. The auto was a green 1985 Chevrolet Celebrity. The bus with 15 passengers was traveling south on Jay Street. The bus had a green traffic light in its favor at the Jay St.-Fulton Street intersection. The bus driver was Art Simmons, badge no. 5712, license number S 24368 35274 263 745-42.

Two passengers in the bus fell onto the floor. An elderly woman (age 65) bruised her left knee. A male (age 25) bruised the palm of his right hand. The auto driver's daughter, Mary (age 19), who was in the right front seat, bumped her head on the windshield. The police and an ambulance were summoned. The three injured persons were taken to Cumberland Hospital by attendant John Hawkins. Police Officer Thomas Brown, badge number 2354, from the 68th Precinct, took statements from witnesses to the accident.

ACCIDENT REPORT

TO BE FILLED IN BY BUS OPERATOR

Route __1__   Run __2__   Vehicle Type: Bus Truck Auto Other Vehicle __3__

T.A. Vehicle No. __4__   T.A. License Plate No. __5__   Make __6__

Date of Accident __7__   Hour __8__   Street Lights On __9__

Place of Accident __10__

Direction of T.A. Vehicle __11__   Direction of Other Vehicle __12__

State if operating on one or two way street. T.A. Vehicle __13__ way.   Other vehicle __14__ way.

Did accident occur in bus stop area? __15__

Number of passengers in T.A. Vehicle __16__   Number of persons in other vehicle __17__

Traffic lights involved __18__   Color of same when leaving near corner __19__

Was ambulance called? __20__   Person taken to what hospital? __21__

Was police officer present? __22__   Officer's No. __23__   Precinct __24__

Name of owner of other vehicle __25__   License No. of other vehicle __26__

Address of owner of other vehicle __27__

Color of other vehicle __28__   Model of other vehicle __29__

Year of other vehicle __30__   Make of other vehicle __31__

Name of driver of other vehicle __32__

Address of driver of other vehicle __33__

License No. of driver of other vehicle __34__

Other driver male or female __35__

BUS OPERATOR IDENTIFYING INFORMATION: PASS #36; BADGE #37; LICENSE #38.

21. Which of the following should be entered in space 4?

    (A) B 67   (B) 12   (C) 7026   (D) 10346 K

22. Which of the following should be entered in space 12?

    (A) north   (B) south   (C) east   (D) west

23. Which of the following should be entered in space 16?

    (A) 10   (B) 12   (C) 15   (D) 67

24. Which of the following should be entered in space 24?

    (A) 62   (B) 67   (C) 68   (D) 2354

25. Which of the following should be entered in space 28?

    (A) red   (B) blue   (C) yellow   (D) green

26. Which of the following should be entered in space 32?

    (A) Martha Ryan   (C) George Ryan
    (B) Mary Ryan   (D) John Hawkins

27. Which of the following should be entered in space 37?

    (A) 2354   (B) 5712   (C) 51 VOM-NY   (D) 5127

28. An angry passenger scolds Bus Operator George Smith for not stopping at a bus stop. Smith did not hear the passenger signal, but there was a lot of traffic noise and he realizes the passenger might have signalled. Of the following, the best action for the bus operator to take is to

    (A) keep driving, say nothing, and stop at the next bus stop for which he hears a signal
    (B) stop the bus immediately and let the passenger off
    (C) tell the passenger in no uncertain terms to signal clearly in the future and, as a lesson to the passenger, skip the next stop as well
    (D) explain that he did not hear a signal and let the passenger off at the next stop

29. As a bus approaches a crowded bus stop, an elderly passenger sitting with a cane near the front of the bus rings the bell to get off. Which of the following is the best action for the bus driver to take?

    (A) Stop short of the bus stop, let the elderly passenger out the front door, then pull into the bus stop.
    (B) Pull into the bus stop, open the front and rear doors and tell the elderly passenger to walk to the rear door to get off.
    (C) Pull into the bus stop, open the doors and tell the crowd, "Please let this passenger off."
    (D) Pull into the bus stop, let the crowd on first, then permit the elderly passenger to get out the front door.

30. At an intersection with no traffic control device, which of the following has the right-of-way over the others?

    (A) a pedestrian in a crosswalk
    (B) a vehicle making a right turn
    (C) a vehicle approaching the intersection
    (D) a bus crossing the intersection

40 / Bus Operator

Questions 31 through 35 should be answered solely on the basis of the EXCLUSIVE LANE RULES printed below.

EXCLUSIVE LANE RULES

Bus Operators using the exclusive bus and taxi lane westbound to the Howard Tunnel in the eastbound roadway of the Porter Expressway should be guided by the following rules:

1. Headlights must be turned on just before entering the bus lane.

2. Speed must not exceed 35 miles per hour. Police will enforce this limit.

3. At least a 200-foot spacing must be maintained behind the vehicle ahead.

4. If a traffic cone is in the lane, drive over it. Do not attempt to go around it and do not stop your bus.

5. Lane hours are only from 7:00 A.M. to 10:00 A.M. Do not enter at any other time or if the lane is closed.

6. Do not leave the lane at any time, not even to pass a disabled vehicle, except under police direction.

7. Do not open doors or discharge passengers from a disabled bus until police assistance has arrived.

8. Any Transit Authority bus in the exclusive lane able to accommodate discharged passengers from a disabled bus of *any* company will do so without requiring payment of additional fare.

31. Transit Authority Bus Operator James Hanzelik is operating his bus in the exclusive bus and taxi lane. He is carrying 25 passengers and has room for about 40 more. Hanzelik comes upon an Antelope Bus Company bus which has broken down in front of him in his lane. The Antelope bus has 20 passengers in it. Hanzelik stops his bus. A short time later, a police officer arrives on the scene. Bus Operator Hanzelik should pass the disabled bus under the direction of the police officer after first

    (A) taking on the passengers from the disabled bus without charge
    (B) taking on the passengers of the disabled bus and charging each of them the difference between the Transit Authority fare and the Antelope Bus Company fare
    (C) politely declining to take on the passengers of the disabled bus because it is not a Transit Authority bus
    (D) taking on the passengers of the disabled bus and charging each of them the regular Transit Authority fare

32. You are driving a bus in the exclusive bus and taxi lane. If you observe a traffic cone in the middle of your lane you should

    (A) stop your bus and place the traffic cone where it belongs
    (B) go around the traffic cone to avoid destroying it
    (C) drive over the traffic cone
    (D) call for the police to move the traffic cone

33. Bus Operator Peter Globe is traveling in the exclusive bus and taxi lane when his bus becomes disabled. He stops his bus in the lane and phones for police assistance. While he is waiting for the police to arrive, another bus in the same lane pulls up behind him. The second bus has enough room to accommodate his passengers. After consulting with the other bus operator, he transfers his passengers to the second bus without charging an additional fare. Bus Operator Globe's action was

    (A) proper, because the other bus had sufficient room to accommodate his passengers
    ✓(B) improper, because he transferred the passengers without police assistance
    (C) proper, because both buses stayed in the exclusive lane
    (D) improper, because he did not charge his passengers an additional fare

34. A bus operator driving his bus legally in the exclusive bus and taxi lane should have his headlights on

    (A) only when he is passing another vehicle
    (B) only when the driver ahead is driving too slowly
    (C) if his speed exceeds 35 miles per hour
    ✓(D) at all times

35. Bus Operator Hector Gonzalez is driving his bus in the exclusive bus lane when he has to stop because of a disabled auto blocking his way. The auto had been traveling eastbound in the next lane but got a flat tire and came to a stop in the exclusive lane. Gonzalez waits until the police arrive to guide him around the disabled auto. After the police guide Gonzalez around the disabled auto, they leave. In order to reach the Howard Tunnel before 10:00 A.M., Bus Operator Gonzalez drives at 40 miles an hour and keeps a distance of 250 feet behind a taxi. He arrives at the Howard Tunnel without incident. His action was

    (A) proper, because the lane hours are from 7:00 A.M. to 10:00 A.M.
    ✓(B) improper, because his speed exceeded 35 miles per hour
    (C) proper, because he made up for lost time in maintaining his schedule
    (D) improper, because he should not have waited for the police to guide him

Answer questions 36 and 37 solely on the basis of the information contained in the following two rules.

1. Bus operators must be relieved only at designated relief points and at the time specified in schedules, unless otherwise instructed by the proper authority. They must never leave their bus until properly relieved, and must not, under any circumstances, surrender the bus to another employee apparently unfit for duty.

2. If a passenger becomes disorderly, annoying, or dangerous, this passenger must be asked to leave the bus at the next designated bus stop.

36. Bus Operator Herbert Bacon is worried about his teen-aged daughter who underwent a serious operation. He wants to phone his wife at the hospital to find out how his daughter is feeling. At a designated bus stop he parks the bus and goes into a tobacco store to use the public telephone. His action was

    (A) proper, because he parked in a designated bus stop
    (B) improper, because he left the bus with no bus operator in charge
    (C) proper, because the nature of the situation justified the phone call
    (D) improper, because he could have used a telephone in the street

42 / Bus Operator

37. Bus Operator Wendy Green notices that a passenger who is obviously drunk is annoying the other passengers with his loud and embarrassing remarks. She asks him several times to be quiet, but he continues to bother the passengers. Bus Operator Green should stop the bus

    (A) immediately and ask the drunken passenger to get off
    (B) at the the next dispatcher's station and ask the drunken passenger to get off
    (C) at the next red light and ask the drunken passenger to get off
    (D) at the next designated bus stop and ask the drunken passenger to get off

38. Oak Street is one-way northbound and is intersected by Elm Street which is one-way eastbound. If there are no traffic control devices at the intersection, and if traffic allows, it should be permissible to make a

    (A) right turn from Elm Street into Oak Street
    (B) right turn from Oak Street into Elm Street
    (C) left turn from Oak Street into Elm Street
    (D) four corner U-turn at the intersection

Questions 39 through 46 should be answered by consulting the Bus Map on the previous page. Notice that the left edge of the map is divided into spaces with letters, and the bottom edge of the map is divided into spaces with numbers. The lines for a space with a letter and the lines for a space with a number if extended across the map would meet and form a quadrant (or area). As an example, look at the sketch below which represents part of the map and note that the quadrant formed by an extension of the lines which are the boundaries of the F space and of the 2 space meet to form the F2 quadrant. The locations referred to in the questions below can be found within the quadrants shown in parentheses.

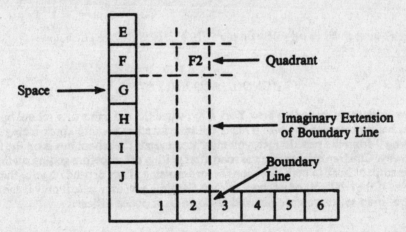

39. Which bus route goes from Stuyvesant Square (quadrant A5) to Abingdon Square (quadrant A2)?

    (A) 15 (B) 9 (C) 14 (D) 10

40. Which bus route goes from the 34th Street Heliport (quadrant B5) to the Circle Line Ferry Terminal at Pier 83 (quadrant C1)?

    (A) 34 (B) 42 (C) 16 (D) 15

41. Which bus route goes from Columbus Circle (quadrant D2) to the Roosevelt Island Tramway (quadrant C5)?

    (A) 103 (B) 7 (C) 6 (D) 32

44 / Bus Operator

42. Which bus route goes from the Port Authority Bus Terminal (quadrant C2) to the United Nations (quadrant C5)?

    (A) 10   (B) 6   (C) 16   (D) 42

43. Which bus route goes from Rockefeller Center (quadrant C3) to Lincoln Center (quadrant D2)?

    (A) 30   (B) 7   (C) 32   (D) 6

44. Which bus route goes from Times Square (quadrant C3) to Union Square (quadrant A4)?

    (A) 10   (B) 6 only   (C) 7 only   (D) 6 and 7

45. Which bus route goes from the New York Public Library (quadrant C3) to Penn Station (quadrant B3)?

    (A) 4   (B) 5   (C) 1   (D) 7

46. Which bus route goes from Sutton Place (quadrant D5) to De Witt Clinton Park (quadrant C1)?

    (A) 32   (B) 30   (C) 28   (D) 11

Answer questions 47 through 49 based solely on the *SCHOOL BUS BULLETIN* below.

SCHOOL BUS BULLETIN

Anywhere in New York State, including New York City, when the red lights of a school bus flash, you must stop your vehicle before reaching the bus. This is the law, whether you are approaching the bus from the front, or overtaking it from the rear. In fact, you must stop even if the school bus is on the far side of a four-lane divided highway. Children might cross the road after getting off or before getting on the school bus, and they don't always stop to check in both directions before crossing. They depend on you, the motorist, to stop as the law requires. If the red lights of a school bus are flashing, you may pass it only if the school bus driver clearly signals you to do so, or you are directed to do so by a police officer.

47. It is evening rush hour during a very hot day. The bus you are operating is 15 minutes behind schedule because of very heavy traffic. The air conditioning system in your bus has broken down and your passengers are uncomfortable, annoyed, and anxious to get home. You are on a wide, two-way street, and you approach a school bus which is parked with its red lights flashing on the other side of the street. The school bus driver is at the wheel, but you see no children in the bus or anywhere on the street. Under the circumstances you should

    (A) proceed with caution past the school bus
    (B) proceed with normal speed past the school bus
    (C) stop your bus before reaching the school bus
    (D) radio for a police officer to direct you past the school bus

48. You are a bus operator on a two-lane, one-way main street. You are in the left lane stopped in back of an automobile at a red light. In the lane to your right and in front of you is a school bus which is also waiting for the red light to change. There is no police officer at the corner. When the light changes to green, the car in front of you moves through the intersection, but the school bus stalls and will not start. It does not flash its red lights. Under the circumstances you

    (A) may pass the school bus because its red lights are not flashing
    (B) may not pass the school bus because there may be children in it
    (C) may pass the school bus only if the school bus driver signals for you to do so
    (D) may not pass the school bus because there is no police officer on the scene

49. You are operating a Transit Authority bus on a one-way street. You approach a school bus from the rear. It is parked at the right curb with its red lights flashing. The school bus is almost filled with children, although a few more are waiting on the sidewalk to get on. After you stop your bus, the school bus driver who is seated at the wheel of the bus, signals you to pass on the left. Under the circumstances, it would be

    (A) proper for you to pass the school bus, because its driver signalled for you to do so
    (B) improper for you to pass the school bus, because children were still boarding
    (C) proper for you to pass the school bus, because most of the children were already inside the bus
    (D) improper for you to pass the school bus, because its red lights were flashing

Answer questions 50 through 52 solely on the basis of the bulletin shown below.

COLORS OF MONTHLY ELEMENTARY AND REDUCED FARE SCHOOL TICKETS — SUMMER 1989

For the Summer of 1989, the colors of the tickets for the School Fare Program for school children will be as follows:

MONTHLY ELEMENTARY SCHOOL TICKETS

Elementary pass FREE — no payment of fare required.

    July   1989   Blue With Blue Date
    August   1989   Rose With Blue Date

HIGH SCHOOL ELIGILIBITY CARDS

Students will pay 50¢ going to school in the A.M. and 50¢ on the return trip from school in the P.M. the entire Summer Session.

    July   1989   Beige (Green "S")
    August   1989   Yellow (Green "S")

TYPE #2 (r) & #3 (c) RAPID TRANSIT SURFACE EXTENSION

High School students presenting reduced fare passes for all Rapid Transit Surface Extension Routes — B/42, B/54, B/35, BX/55, and Q/49 will be required to pay $1.00 in the A.M. on the way to school for the entire Summer Session, July 6, 1989 through August 14, 1989.

50. Joe is a second year high school student attending the Summer Session. If he boards a bus on Wednesday, July 23,

    (A) he can ride free is he has a valid Blue ticket with Blue Date
    (B) he must pay 50¢ and show a Beige (Green "S") card
    (C) he must pay 50¢ and show a Blue (Green "C") card
    (D) he must pay 50¢ and show a Yellow (Green "S") card

51. Mary is a senior in high school attending the Summer Session. When she boards the Surface Extension Route B/54 on her way to taking the train to school, she must show her reduced fare pass and pay

    (A) no fare   (B) 50¢   (C) $1.00   (D) 90¢

52. George, a junior in high school, and his brother, Tyrone, in 5th grade, are both attending the Summer Session. If they board a bus on Tuesday, August 4th, the bus operator should look for

    (A) a rose ticket and a yellow card
    (B) a blue ticket and a beige card
    (C) a blue ticket and a blue card
    (D) a rose ticket and a beige card

53. You are a bus operator driving your bus at normal route speed. Suddenly, a man in a sports car cuts sharply in front of you and continues to speed away from you. Which of the following actions would it be best for you to take now?

    (A) Accelerate to catch up to the sports car, then cut it off.
    (B) Get the license number of the sports car and radio a report to the police.
    (C) Slow down until the sports car is at least a quarter mile ahead of you.
    (D) Continue along your route at normal speed.

Answer questions 54 through 56 solely on the basis of the *REVERSE BUS MOVEMENT PROCEDURE* printed below.

REVERSE BUS MOVEMENT PROCEDURE

Bus operators may operate a bus in reverse only if they determine that no other turn or movement is possible. When operating in reverse, bus operators must follow all of the following steps in this procedure.

1. The movement in reverse must not be made until the bus operator has walked around to the back of the bus and made a visual inspection of the area behind the bus.

2. The bus operator must be guided by a responsible person, such as a police officer or another bus driver.

3. The person guiding the bus operator must station himself near the left rear of the bus.

4. When the bus operator has determined that it is safe to back up, he will signal by giving three toots of the horn immediately before starting the reverse movement.

54. Bus Operator Charles Waters has stopped directly behind a disabled bus and cannot move around the bus without backing up. Waters remains in his seat and asks a police officer to stand at the left rear of the bus to direct him. Waters toots his horn three times and slowly backs up just enough to go around the disabled bus. Bus Operator Waters' actions in backing up the bus were improper because Waters

(A) was not guided by a responsible person
(B) should have gotten permission from a supervisor before backing up
(C) tooted his horn just before backing up
(D) did not inspect the area behind the bus before backing up

55. Bus Operator Elaine Strollin determines that it is necessary to operate her bus in reverse. She inspects the area to the rear of her bus and determines that it is safe to back up. She toots her horn three times to attract the attention of a police officer to assist her in backing up the bus. The police officer goes to the proper position to direct Operator Strollin. With the passengers still in her bus, Operator Strollin is directed by the police officer and backs up her bus without incident. Operator Strollin's actions in backing up the bus were

(A) proper, because she had followed the complete procedure for a reverse bus movement
(B) improper, because she did not discharge her passengers before backing up
(C) proper, because with a police officer present the complete procedure for a reverse bus movement need not be followed
(D) improper, because she did not toot her horn three times just before backing up

56. A bus operator has decided that he must back up his bus. The operator has asked a responsible person to guide his bus back. Where should he ask that person to stand?

(A) in front of the bus
(B) on the right side of the bus near the front door
(C) at the left rear of the bus
(D) at the right rear of the bus

57. A careful driver should allow 20 feet of stopping room for each ten miles an hour of speed. When driving at night you should be able to stop within the roadway distance illuminated by your headlights. If your headlights illuminate the roadway approximately 90 feet before you, your speed at night should not exceed about

(A) 25 miles per hour
(B) 35 miles per hour
(C) 45 miles per hour
(D) 55 miles per hour

Answer questions 58 and 59 based on the bulletin shown in part below.

The Culture Bus Loops operate on Saturdays, Sundays, and some holidays. The buses on Culture Loop I (M41) run on the loop through midtown and uptown Manhattan every 30 minutes during the winter, and every 20 minutes during the summer, from 10:00 A.M. to 6:00 P.M. and make 22 stops. You may get off at any one of the stops, take in the sights, and then catch a later bus, or you can simply stay on the bus for the entire loop. Culture Bus Loop II (B88) provides another view of New York City, one that includes midtown and lower Manhattan, and some of Brooklyn as well. The buses on this loop run every 30 minutes, from 9:00 A.M. to 6:00 P.M. Running time is approximately 2 hours and 25 minutes. Tickets for the Culture Buses may be bought only on the buses. Since the driver cannot make change, and since our fare boxes will not accept paper currency, please have your $2.50 fare in any combination of coins or tokens and coins. The Culture Bus Loop I ticket is valid for certain transfer privileges to crosstown buses. By using the crosstown buses you may tailor your day's itinerary. The Culture Bus Loop I ticket is also valid as an extension to and from the Cloisters on the M4 bus from Stop 10.

58. The Culture Loop II bus (B88) goes into which borough or boroughs?

    (A) Brooklyn and Manhattan
    (B) Brooklyn and Queens
    (C) Manhattan only
    (D) Manhattan and the Bronx

59. The Culture Bus Loop I ticket is also valid on the M4 bus as an extension to and from

    (A) Brooklyn Heights
    (B) the Cloisters
    (C) Greenwich Village
    (D) Staten Island

60. A bus that is traveling at 22 MPH with 30 passengers has a green light as it approaches an intersection. Just as the bus enters the intersection, the light changes from green to yellow. Which of the following is the best action for the bus operator to take?

    (A) Stop short, back his bus out of the intersection, wait for the light to turn green again, then drive through the intersection.
    (B) Stop quickly, wait in the intersection for the light to turn green again, then drive through the intersection.
    (C) Continue through the intersection at 22 MPH.
    (D) Speed up to get through the intersection before the light turns red.

61. You are driving your bus down a one-way street during the rush hour and you are already 5 minutes behind schedule. You find that you must stop your bus because the street is blocked by a parcel delivery truck which is double parked, and the driver is not in sight. Which of the following is the first action you should take?

    (A) Try to attract the attention of the truck driver by blowing your horn.
    (B) Back the bus out of the street.
    (C) Radio the police for a tow truck to come and haul away the parcel delivery truck.
    (D) Jump out of the bus and knock on the door of the house nearest to the parked truck.

62. A bus operator is behind schedule. He has closed his doors and is about to pull out of a bus stop and cross an intersection. The green light is about to change. An elderly man raps on the door of the bus. The operator realizes that if he opens the door for the man to board he will miss the light and get even further behind schedule. Which of the following is the best action for the bus operator to take?

    (A) Pull away from the bus stop and continue on his route.
    (B) Go through the intersection before the light changes, then wait for the elderly man to cross the street and board the bus.
    (C) Open the door and let the man board the bus.
    (D) Open the door, let the man onto the bus, and tell the man he should have waited for the next bus.

Answer questions 63 and 64 solely on the basis of the information contained in the bulletin shown below on air pollution.

AIR POLLUTION

No bus operator should permit the gasoline or diesel engine of his bus to discharge air-polluting gases while the bus is stationary at a route terminal. Operators must shut off bus engines, unless otherwise directed, *immediately upon completing arrival at the terminal stop*. All operators and supervisors should remain constantly alert for any Transit Authority vehicles emitting excessive fumes while in motion. They should report such vehicles immediately on their bus radios to Surface Control by bus number together with any further available identifying information.

SECOND SAMPLE EXAM

Bus Operator

DIRECTIONS: Each question has four suggested answers, lettered A, B, C, and D. Decide which one is the best answer and, on the sample answer sheet, find the question number which corresponds to the answer that you have selected. Darken the area with a soft pencil.

The time allowed for the entire examination is 3 hours.

1. Most of the north-and-south avenues in Manhattan have been changed from two-way to one-way traffic. The primary reason for making this change is that

    (A) curb parking space is greatly increased
    (B) traffic can move along the avenues with fewer delays
    (C) pedestrian crossing is made much easier
    (D) cleaning of the avenues is made easier

2. Present traffic procedure is to have one lane on many wide one-way streets marked out in yellow paint. This lane is to be

    (A) used by regular vehicles when a siren is heard
    (B) cleared for vehicles about to make a left turn
    (C) used exclusively by emergency vehicles
    (D) cleared for emergency vehicles when a siren is heard

3. A bus operator need *not* pull over to the curb and come to a stop

    (A) when signaled to do so by a policeman
    (B) at a bus stop where passengers are waiting
    (C) at the sound of a fire engine siren
    (D) when he hears the horn of the car behind

4. The New York City Transit Authority maintains a lost property office at 370 Jay Street, Brooklyn. The establishment of such an office

    (A) insures the return of all lost articles
    (B) encourages the turning in of lost articles by the finders
    (C) simplifies the return to owners of lost articles turned in
    (D) discourages loss of articles

53

5. To stop a motor vehicle on an icy street with the least chance of skidding, the operator should

   (A) apply the brakes normally
   (B) step on the accelerator lightly after releasing it
   (C) make a number of light foot-brake applications
   (D) apply the hand brake only

6. Passengers must have the correct fare ready when boarding a bus mainly because this

   (A) assures collection of all fares
   (B) permits a fuller bus load
   (C) makes the job more attractive
   (D) reduces the commission of crime on buses

7. Transit employees are urged to be courteous to passengers mainly to

   (A) assure safety
   (B) maintain bus schedules
   (C) win prizes
   (D) maintain good public relations

8. Improper use of the horn of a motor vehicle is not permitted. It would be clearly improper for a bus operator to sound

   (A) several short blasts to warn pedestrian stragglers in front of his bus at an intersection
   (B) several short blasts to warn a motorist about to pull away from the curb in front of a moving bus
   (C) three short blasts as a warning before he backs up
   (D) two short blasts as he is passing another bus going in the opposite direction

9. A recognized principle in good urban transportation is that the interval between buses at any particular time of day should be uniform. The most likely consequences of an unusually long time gap between buses resulting from traffic conditions is

   (A) heavy riding on some buses
   (B) confusion of passengers
   (C) crossing accidents
   (D) loss of regular patronage

10. Safety rules are most useful because they

    (A) are a guide to avoid common dangers
    (B) prevent carelessness
    (C) fix responsibility for accidents
    (D) make it unnecessary to think

11. It is an indication of a safe driver if the operator

    (A) seldom yields the right-of-way
    (B) seldom runs ahead of schedule
    (C) frequently yields the right-of-way
    (D) frequently runs behind schedule

12. A person who has been a rider on buses in New York City can reason that the failure which would *least* likely be the cause for a bus being taken out of service is a

    (A) rear door stuck closed
    (B) front door stuck closed
    (C) rear door stuck open
    (D) front door stuck open

13. The vehicular tunnel that can be operated so as to have more lanes in the direction of heaviest traffic is the

    (A) Holland
    (B) Lincoln
    (C) Brooklyn-Battery
    (D) Queens-Midtown

Questions 14 to 23 inclusive are based on the description of an incident given below. Read the description carefully before answering these questions.

DESCRIPTION OF ACCIDENT

On Tuesday, October 10, 1989, at about 4:00 P.M., bus operator Sam Bell, badge No. 38F1, whose accident record was perfect, was operating his half-filled bus, No. 4392Y, northbound and on schedule along Dean Street. At this time, a male passenger who was apparently intoxicated started to yell and to use loud and profane language. The bus driver told this passenger to be quiet or to get off the bus. The passenger said that he would not be quiet but indicated that he wanted to get off the bus by moving toward the front door exit. When he reached the front of the bus, which at the time was in motion, the intoxicated passenger slapped the bus operator on the back and pulled the steering wheel sharply. This action caused the bus to sideswipe a passenger automobile coming from the opposite direction before the operator could stop the bus. The sideswiped car was a red 1985 Pontiac 2-door sedan, New York License 6416-KN, driven by Albert Holt. The bus driver kept the doors of his bus closed and blew the horn vigorously. The horn blowing was quickly answered as sergeant Henry Burns, badge No. 1208, and patrolman Joe Cross, badge No. 24643, happened to be following a few cars behind the bus in police car No. 736. The intoxicated passenger, who gave his name as John Doe, was placed under arrest, and patrolman Cross took the names of witnesses while sergeant Burns recorded the necessary vehicular information. Investigation showed that no one was injured in the accident and that the entire damage to the automobile was having its side slightly pushed in.

14. From the information given, it can be reasoned that

    (A) it was just beginning to rain
    (B) Dean Street is a two-way street
    (C) there were mostly women shoppers on the bus
    (D) most seats in the bus were filled

15. The name of the policeman who was riding in the police car with the sergeant was

    (A) Cross
    (B) Bell
    (C) Holt
    (D) Burns

16. From the description, it is evident that the passenger automobile was travelling

    (A) north
    (B) south
    (C) east
    (D) west

17. It is logical to conclude that the passenger automobile was damaged on its

    (A) front end
    (B) rear end
    (C) right side
    (D) left side

18. A fact concerning the intoxicated passenger that is clearly stated in the above description is that he

    (A) was intoxicated when he got on the bus
    (B) hit a fellow passenger
    (C) pulled the steering wheel sharply
    (D) was not arrested

19. The bus operator called the attention of the police by

    (A) sideswiping an oncoming car
    (B) yelling and using profane language
    (C) blowing his horn vigorously
    (D) stopping a police car coming from the opposite direction

20. A reasonable conclusion that can be drawn from the above description is that

    (A) the name John Doe was fictitious
    (B) the sideswiped automobile was from out of town
    (C) some of the passengers on the bus were injured
    (D) the bus operator tried to put the intoxicated passenger off the bus

21. The number of the police car involved in the incident was

    (A) 4392Y
    (B) 6416-KN
    (C) 1208
    (D) 736

22. From the facts stated, it is obvious that the bus operator was

    (A) behind schedule
    (B) driving too close to the center of the street
    (C) discourteous to the intoxicated passenger
    (D) a good driver

23. It is clearly stated that the

    (A) sideswiped automobile was a blue sedan
    (B) bus driver kept the bus doors closed until the police came
    (C) incident happened on a Thursday
    (D) police sergeant took down the names of witnesses

24. At terminals in residential areas where a bus remains for more than 3 minutes, operators are required to turn off their engines. The *least* important reason for stopping the engines is to

    (A) reduce noise
    (B) conserve fuel
    (C) reduce air pollution
    (D) minimize engine wear

25. Statistics show that automobile accidents occur most frequently

    (A) in the morning rush hours
    (B) around noon
    (C) soon after sunset
    (D) near midnight

26. A bus operator is liable under the law to receive a traffic ticket for

    (A) double standing when a bus stop is occupied by a car
    (B) not taking on all people waiting at a stop
    (C) passing a preceding bus on a grade
    (D) discharging a passenger at other than a bus stop

27. A bus operator approaching a green light sees a pedestrian crossing his path against the light. If the pedestrian is two or three bus lengths away, the operator

    (A) is required to make a complete stop
    (B) should swing his bus closer to the curb
    (C) is required to report the pedestrian to the nearest police officer
    (D) should reduce his speed and blow his horn

28. Bus operators have been instructed to confiscate reduced fare cards for any one of the following acts on the part of a student: 1, misbehavior; 2, vandalism; 3, passing card to another student; 4, using card during unauthorized hours. On this basis, a student caught cutting the seats of a bus with a penknife would have his card lifted for reason number

    (A) 1
    (B) 2
    (C) 3
    (D) 4

29. The power to revoke a license to drive a motor vehicle is in the hands of the

    (A) Police Commissioner
    (B) Traffic Commissioner
    (C) Commissioner of Motor Vehicles
    (D) Mayor

30. A directive of the transit authority instructs operators to accept, without comment, tokens deposited in the fare box or presented by passengers unable to pay fare in cash, and under no circumstances to sell tokens or exchange tokens for cash. This implies that, in respect to tokens collected, operators are to

(A) use them in making change
(B) return them to passengers depositing them and request cash
(C) keep them and turn them in with the day's receipts
(D) offer them for cash to passengers going to the subway

31. The bridge which does *not* have two vehicular levels is the

(A) Brooklyn
(B) George Washington
(C) Manhattan
(D) Queensborough

Questions 32 to 41 inclusive are based on the sketch below showing the routes of the Grand Avenue (solid line) and the Elm Street (dotted line) buses. Refer to this sketch when answering these questions.

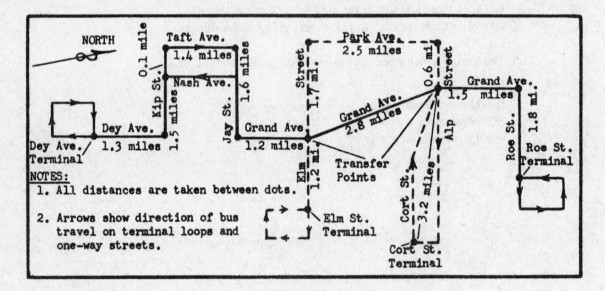

32. A bus on Alp Street going to the Cort Street terminal is moving

    (A) north
    (B) east
    (C) south
    (D) west

33. If the distance around a terminal loop is one-half mile, the total distance that a bus must travel in one round trip between the Dey Avenue and Roe Street terminals, including both terminal loops is nearest to

    (A) 26.2 miles
    (B) 26.7 miles
    (C) 27.2 miles
    (D) 28.4 miles

34. One street used by buses operating in both directions is

    (A) Taft Avenue
    (B) Roe Street
    (C) Cort Street
    (D) Nash Avenue

35. The bus route distance between the Elm Street and Cort Street terminals is

(A) 8.6 miles
(B) 9.2 miles
(C) 9.7 miles
(D) 13.9 miles

36. A passenger must transfer if he is going from Dey Avenue terminal to

(A) Taft Avenue
(B) Elm Street
(C) Cort Street
(D) Park Avenue

37. Buses are *not* required to make even one left turn at the terminal at

(A) Cort Street
(B) Dey Avenue
(C) Elm Street
(D) Roe Street

38. After discharging all passengers at the Dey Avenue terminal before going around the loop, the number of left turns a bus must make to reach Elm Street is

(A) 1
(B) 2
(C) 3
(D) 4

39. From the Cort Street terminal to Elm Street, a bus travels a total distance of

(A) 5.7 miles
(B) 6.0 miles
(C) 6.3 miles
(D) 7.2 miles

40. If the common rule for estimating distance of 20 blocks to the mile is adhered to, then the number of blocks a bus travels on Grand Avenue is

(A) 56
(B) 80
(C) 110
(D) 136

41. If the timetable calls for a bus to cover the distance along Dey Avenue from the terminal to Kip Street in 12 minutes, the average speed of the bus on this stretch must be

(A) 1.1 miles per hour
(B) 6.5 miles per hour
(C) 10 miles per hour
(D) 15.5 miles per hour

42. When summoning an ambulance for an injured person it is most important to give

    (A) the place where he may be found
    (B) the cause of the accident
    (C) his name and address
    (D) a detailed account of his injuries

43. If a person should ask you, while on duty in your bus, for directions on how to reach a particular location to which you do not know the answer, your best course of action is to

    (A) tell the person you do not know
    (B) give the person the best directions you can think of
    (C) tell the person to buy a directory
    (D) explain to the person that the rules prohibit talking to an operator while he is on duty

44. The rules of the transit authority state that employees should not make any statements concerning transit accidents except to proper officials of the transit authority upon inquiry. The probable reason for this rule is to

    (A) conceal facts that may be damaging
    (B) avoid conflicting testimony
    (C) prevent lawsuits
    (D) prevent unofficial statements from being accepted as official

45. As a potential bus operator you should know that when you are about to back a bus it is *never* necessary for you to

    (A) check that there is sufficient room behind the bus
    (B) signal your intention
    (C) turn on back-up lights
    (D) check the brake air pressure

46. A flashing red traffic signal indicates that a driver

    (A) must stop and wait until the light stops flashing
    (B) must stop and then proceed when the way is clear
    (C) may make a right turn without stopping
    (D) must yield the right-of-way but does not have to stop

47. Operators should be instructed that collision accidents at street intersections protected by traffic lights can usually be avoided if they will remember that

    (A) traffic lights are often out of order
    (B) a car coming from the right has the right-of-way
    (C) they can depend on the other driver obeying the lights
    (D) there is no substitute for an alert driver

48. Passengers should not be permitted to rest their feet on the seats of buses because

   (A) disease is spread in that way
   (B) to do so is an indication of bad manners
   (C) they may cause damage to the property of the transit system
   (D) it always prevents other passengers from being seated

49. The weekly pay for 8 hours a day, 5 days a week, at $8.6250 an hour can be calculated as

   (A) 5 × 8 × 8.2650
   (B) 8 + 5 × 8.6250
   (C) 8 × 5 × 8.6250
   (D) 8 + 5 × 8.5260

Questions 50 to 59 inclusive are based on the portion of a bus timetable show below. Refer to this timetable in answering these questions.

	TIMETABLE—LAKESIDE LINE—WEEKDAYS							
	SOUTHBOUND				NORTHBOUND			
Bus No.	Mack St. Lv.	High St. Lv.	Ace St. Lv.	Burr St. Arr.	Burr St. Lv.	Ace St. Lv.	High St. Lv.	Mack St. Arr.
10	6:06	6:14	6:32	6:46	6:55	7:09	7:27	7:35
11	6:21	6:29	6:47	7:01	7:10	7:24	7:42	7:50
12	6:36	6:44	7:02	7:16	7:25	7:39	7:57	8:05
13	6:51	6:59	7:17	7:31	7:40	7:54	8:12	8:20
14	7:03	7:11	7:29	7:43	7:55	8:09	8:27	8:35
15	7:15	7:23	7:41	7:55	8:10	8:24	8:42	8:50
16	7:28	7:36	7:54	8:08	8:25	8:39	8:57	9:05
17	7:41	7:49	8:07	8:21L	—	—	—	—
10	7:51	7:59	8:17	8:31	8:40	8:54	9:12	9:20
18	P8:01	8:09	8:27	8:41	8:55	9:09	9:27	9:35
11	8:09	8:17	8:35	8:49L	—	—	—	—
19	P8:17	8:25	8:43	8:57	9:10	9:24	9:42	9:50
12	8:25	8:33	8:51	9:05L	—	—	—	—
20	P8:33	8:41	8:59	9:13	9:25	9:39	9:57	10:05
13	8:43	8:51	9:09	9:23L	—	—	—	—
14	8:58	9:06	9:24	9:38	9:40	9:54	10:12	10:20

Notes: 1. The time interval between buses at a given point is called the headway.
2. The time interval between the arrival and departure of a bus at a terminal is called its layover.
3. P indicates that a bus not already in passenger service is placed in service at the time and place shown.
4. L indicates that a bus is taken out of passenger service at the time and place shown and is sent to the garage.
5. Lv. means "leave," and Arr. means "arrive."

50. The minimum headway shown between buses leaving Mack Street is

    (A) 8 minutes
    (B) 10 minutes
    (C) 12 minutes
    (D) 15 minutes

51. The actual scheduled running time from Burr Street to High Street is

    (A) 14 minutes
    (B) 32 minutes
    (C) 40 minutes
    (D) 64 minutes

52. The layover time for bus No. 16 at Burr Street is

    (A) 9 minutes
    (B) 12 minutes
    (C) 15 minutes
    (D) 17 minutes

53. Bus No. 13 is scheduled to

    (A) follow bus No. 12 from Burr Street to Mack Street, northbound
    (B) leave Ace Street exactly 20 minutes after it leaves Mack Street, southbound
    (C) leave Burr Street for the garage after 8:49
    (D) be placed in service to begin its day run at Mack Street at 8:09

54. The time shown in the timetable for any bus to make the run from Mack Street to Burr Street and return is

    (A) 40 minutes plus the layover time at Burr Street
    (B) 40 minutes minus the layover time at Burr Street
    (C) 80 minutes minus the layover time at Burr Street
    (D) 80 minutes plus the layover time at Burr Street

55. The total number of northbound buses passing High Street between 8:00 and 8:45 is

    (A) 2
    (B) 3
    (C) 4
    (D) 5

56. The total number of buses that is scheduled to leave Mack Street between 7:45 and 8:45 and is also scheduled to return to Mack Street is

    (A) 4
    (B) 5
    (C) 6
    (D) 7

57. The most northerly street on this line is

    (A) Ace Street
    (B) Mack Street
    (C) High Street
    (D) Burr Street

58. A passenger boarding a bus at Burr Street and wishing to get to High Street as close as possible to 9:30, should board the bus which leaves at

    (A) 8:51
    (B) 8:55
    (C) 9:06
    (D) 9:10

59. The number of buses that is shown in the timetable as making two complete round trips is

    (A) 2
    (B) 3
    (C) 5
    (D) 6

60. The two rear wheels of a bus can turn at different speeds when necessary by means of the

    (A) overdrive
    (B) torque converter
    (C) universal joint
    (D) differential

61. If a passenger called a bus operator improper names but took no other action, the bus operator would show good judgment by

    (A) telling the passenger to keep his mouth shut
    (B) acting as if the passenger were not there
    (C) calling the passenger names in return
    (D) driving to the nearest policeman and preferring charges

62. Manuals on driving stress the importance of allowing ample braking distance to the car ahead, the most common rule of thumb being to allow a car length for each ten miles per hour of speed. If the overall length of a car is 210 inches, the proper braking distance to allow at a speed of 40 miles per hour is nearest to

    (A) 700 feet
    (B) 500 feet
    (C) 70 feet
    (D) 50 feet

63. "The safe speed on any road regardless of weather conditions is primarily a function of the ability of the vehicle operator to compensate for roadway and traffic conditions." This statement means most nearly that it is

    (A) always safe to drive well below the posted or allowable speed
    (B) permitted to drive a bus faster than the posted or allowable speed to compensate for traffic delays
    (C) not safe to drive at the maximum posted or allowable speed under any weather conditions
    (D) necessary for a bus operator to use his judgment to determine the safe operating speed

64. If your watch gains 20 minutes per day and you set it to the correct time at 7:00 AM, the correct time, to the nearest minute, when the watch indicates 1:00 P.M. is

    (A) 12:50
    (B) 12:55
    (C) 1:05
    (D) 1:10

65. The law requires that cars having four-wheel brakes must be able to stop in 30 feet from a speed of 20 miles per hour, and in 120 feet from 40 miles per hour. From these requirements and your own knowledge of automobiles in motion, it is most logical to conclude that

    (A) the law is more lenient in regard to fast cars than slow ones
    (B) when speed is doubled the needed braking distance is multiplied by four
    (C) drivers' reactions slow down greatly as speed increases
    (D) any 20 mile per hour increase in speed will require 90 feet more of braking distance

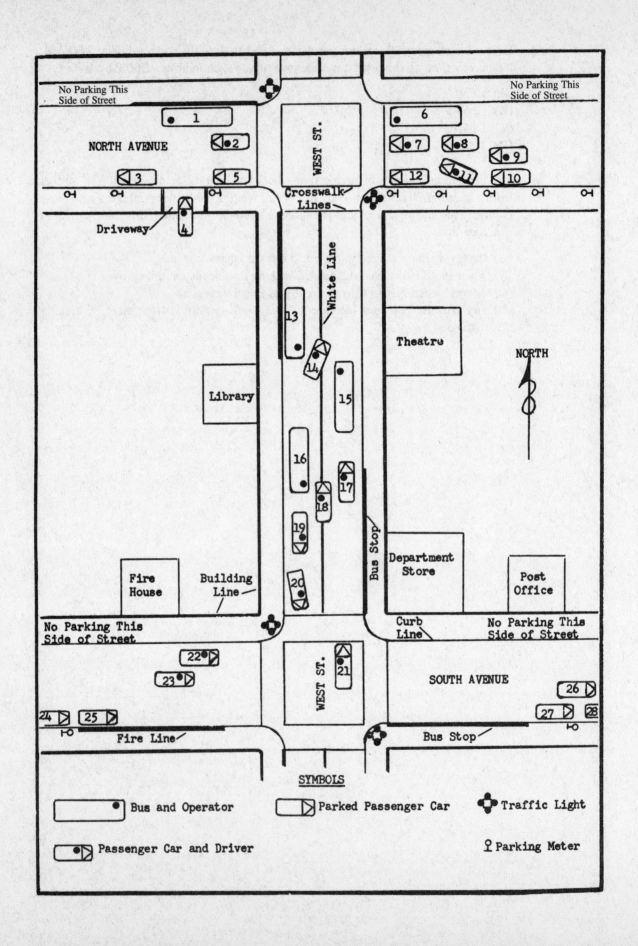

Questions 66 to 74 inclusive are based on the sketch shown on page 68. Refer to this sketch when answering these questions. The sketch shows the situation shortly after the traffic lights have changed to green for north-south traffic and red for east-west traffic.

66. Of the following stopped cars, the one which is in the generally approved position to start to enter a parking space is the one numbered

    (A) 7
    (B) 8
    (C) 9
    (D) 11

67. It is clearly seen that the operator of bus 1 is

    (A) in error in taking up the entire bus stop
    (B) not stopping, as bus 6 will pick up the passengers
    (C) driving in a westerly direction
    (D) ahead of schedule

68. One car which is unquestionably illegally parked is number

    (A) 3
    (B) 10
    (C) 12
    (D) 25

69. The driver of car 4 would be violating the law if he

    (A) stopped at the sidewalk to pick up a passenger
    (B) failed to put on his directional signal for a left turn
    (C) did not blow his horn before crossing the sidewalk
    (D) failed to yield the right-of-way to any vehicle on North Ave. approaching the driveway

70. The car which is in a serious moving violation of the law is number

    (A) 2
    (B) 14
    (C) 17
    (D) 19

71. If cars 22 and 23 are approaching the intersection and the operators of both cars are complying with the law, it is clear that car 22

    (A) is passing car 23
    (B) cannot stop before reaching the intersection
    (C) is in the better position to make a left turn
    (D) will continue across the intersection

72. The driver of car 20 has signaled his intention to make a left turn into South Avenue. The diagram clearly shows that the turn

    (A) was started from too far to the right
    (B) is being made into a heavily traveled street
    (C) is being made at an excessive speed
    (D) can be made regardless of the position of car 21

73. If only a single bus line operates on West Street, it can be reasoned that most likely

    (A) bus 13 is scheduled to follow bus 16
    (B) bus 16 is being taken out of service
    (C) bus 13 is more crowded than bus 16
    (D) bus 16 is ahead of schedule

74. It would be reasonable to infer that most likely

    (A) no parking is allowed on West Street
    (B) the department store is open for business
    (C) West Street is 100 feet wide
    (D) the area shown is primarily residential

THIRD SAMPLE EXAM

Conductor

DIRECTIONS: Choose the best answer to each question and mark its letter, (A), (B), (C), or (D), on your answer sheet.

1. When should an on-the-job accident to a Transit Authority employee be reported to his or her supervisor?

    (A) only if the injury is serious
    (B) as soon as possible
    (C) after the employee is treated at the Transit Authority clinic
    (D) if compensation for injury is called for

2. The proper type of fire-fighting equipment to be used on an electrical fire is a

    (A) soda-acid type extinguisher
    (B) fire hose and water
    (C) dry-chemical type extinguisher
    (D) foam type extinguisher

3. Of the following, the best reason for conductors to be courteous to passengers is to

    (A) discourage vandalism
    (B) speed up train operations
    (C) maintain good public relations
    (D) assure passenger safety

4. The main reason for the Transit Authority's posting commercial advertisements in subway cars is to

    (A) increase the income of the Transit Authority
    (B) help passengers pass time pleasantly on long runs
    (C) make the cars attractive
    (D) inform the passengers about good products

5. Of the following, the best reason why an employee is required to give his or her supervisor a written report of an unusual occurrence immediately is that the

    (A) report may be too lengthy if the employee has more time for writing it
    (B) employee will not be as likely to forget to make the report
    (C) supervisor can keep his reports up-to-date
    (D) report will tend to be more accurate

6. During the rush hour, a passenger asks a conductor on the platform for directions. If the conductor is not sure of the right answer, the conductor should

   (A) tell the passenger to find a public telephone and call train information
   (B) tell the passenger to take the next arriving train and ask that train's conductor
   (C) give the passenger directions that he thinks are right as long as he thinks that the passenger is headed in the right direction
   (D) tell the passenger he isn't sure and suggest that the passenger wait until they can ask the conductor on the next arriving train for the information

7. If a group of teenagers in a subway car is behaving in a disorderly manner, the first thing a conductor should do is to

   (A) request the motorman to call the transit police
   (B) eject this group from the train
   (C) ask this group to quiet down
   (D) refuse to leave the station until this group quiets down

8. Of the following, the best reason for prohibiting the use of intoxicating liquor by employees while on duty is that it may

   (A) make them too active
   (B) make them too talkative
   (C) impair their job performance
   (D) cause them to become ill

9. If a conductor sees a passenger with his feet on a seat, the conductor should

   (A) tell the passenger he will call a transit patrolman
   (B) ignore the situation if the car is not crowded
   (C) stare at him until he puts his feet on the floor
   (D) ask the passenger to please put his feet down

Questions 10 to 13 are based on the Bulletin printed below. Read this Bulletin carefully before answering the questions. Select your answers only on the basis of this Bulletin.

BULLETIN

Rule 107 (m) states in part that "Before closing doors they (conductors) must afford passengers an opportunity to detrain and entrain. . . ."

Doors must be left open long enough to allow passengers to enter and exit from the train. Closing doors on passengers too quickly does not help to shorten the station stop and is a violation of the safety and courtesy which must be accorded to all our passengers.

The proper and effective way to keep passengers moving in and out of the train is to use the public address system. When the train is excessively crowded and passengers on the platform are pushing those in the cars, it may be necessary to close the doors after a reasonable period of time has been allowed.

Closing doors on passengers too quickly is a violation of rules and will be cause for disciplinary actions.

10. Which of the following statements is correct about closing doors on passengers too quickly?

    (A) It will shorten the running time from terminal to terminal.
    (B) It shortens the station stop but is a violation of safety and courtesy.
    (C) It does not help shorten the station stop time.
    (D) It makes the passengers detrain and entrain quicker.

11. The best way to get passengers to move in and out of cars quickly is to

    (A) have the conductors urge passengers to move into doorways
    (B) make announcements over the public address system
    (C) start closing doors while passengers are getting on
    (D) set a fixed time for stopping at each station

12. The conductor should leave doors open at each station stop long enough for passengers to

    (A) squeeze into an excessively crowded train
    (B) get from the local to the express train
    (C) get off and get on the train
    (D) hear the announcements over the public address system

13. Closing doors on passengers too quickly is a violation of rules and is cause for

    (A) the conductor's immediate suspension
    (B) the conductor to be sent back to the terminal for another assignment
    (C) removal of the conductor at the next station
    (D) disciplinary action to be taken against the conductor

Questions 14 to 16 are based on the Bulletin printed below. Read this Bulletin carefully before answering the questions. Select your answers only on the basis of this Bulletin.

BULLETIN

Conductors assigned to train service are not required to wear uniform caps from June 1 to September 30 inclusive.

Conductors assigned to platform duty are required to wear the uniform cap at all times. Conductors are reminded that they must furnish their badge numbers to anyone who requests same.

During the above mentioned period, conductors may remove their uniform coats. The regulation summer short-sleeved shirts must be worn with the regulation uniform trousers. Suspenders are not permitted if the uniform coat is removed. Shoes are to be black, but sandals, sneakers, suede, canvas, or two-tone footwear must not be worn.

Conductors may work without uniform tie if the uniform coat is removed. However, only the top collar button may be opened. The tie may not be removed if the uniform coat is worn.

14. Conductors assigned to platform duty are required to wear uniform caps

    (A) at all times except from July 1 to September 30 inclusive
    (B) whenever they are on duty
    (C) only from June 1 to September 30 inclusive
    (D) only when they remove their uniform coats

15. Suspenders are permitted only if conductors wear

    (A) summer short-sleeved shirts with uniform trousers
    (B) uniform trousers without belt loops
    (C) the type permitted by the Transit Authority
    (D) uniform coats

16. A conductor must furnish his badge number to

    (A) Transit Authority supervisors only
    (B) members of Special Inspection only
    (C) anyone who asks him for it
    (D) passengers only

17. As a train is leaving a station, the conductor notices a passenger being dragged along the platform with his leg caught in a door. The first action the conductor should take is to

    (A) pull the emergency cord
    (B) call the motorman on the public address system
    (C) yell to the platform conductor to pull the man away from the door
    (D) run to the car door holding this passenger and try to help him

18. If a conductor is about to close the door and he sees a passenger with a folded baby carriage hastening to get on the train, he should

    (A) tell the passenger that baby carriages are not allowed on trains
    (B) tell the passenger to hurry up
    (C) hold the doors open long enough to allow the passenger to get on
    (D) hold the doors open no longer than the required 10 seconds

Printed below is part of a Weekday Train Schedule for the Dumont Line. Questions 19 through 26 are based on this schedule. In answering these questions refer only to this schedule.

Weekday Train Schedule – Dumont Line								
Eastbound						Westbound		
Train #	Harvard Square	Pleasure Plaza	Harding Street	Magic Mall		Harding Street	Pleasure Plaza	Harvard Square
	Leave	Leave	Leave	Arrive	Leave	Leave	Leave	Arrive
69	7:48	7:51	7:56	8:00	8:06	8:10	8:15	8:18
70	7:54	7:57	8:02	8:06	8:12	8:16	8:21	8:24
71	8:00	8:03	8:08	8:12	8:18	8:22	8:27	8:30
72	8:04	8:07	8:13	8:17	8:22	8:26	8:31	8:34
73	8:08	8:11	8:17	8:21	8:26	8:30	8:35	8:38
74	8:12	8:15	8:20	8:24	8:30	8:34	8:39	8:42
75	8:16	8:19	8:24	8:28	8:34	8:38	8:43	8:46
69	8:20	8:23	8:28	8:32	8:38	8:42	8:47	8:50
70	8:26	8:29	8:34	8:38	8:44	8:48	8:53	8:56

19. Train #70 is scheduled to leave Pleasure Plaza on its second westbound trip to Harvard Square at

    (A) 7:57
    (B) 8:21
    (C) 8:29
    (D) 8:53

20. The time it should take Train #74 to go from Harvard Square to Magic Mall is

    (A) 8 minutes
    (B) 12 minutes
    (C) 18 minutes
    (D) 30 minutes

21. As shown on this schedule, the number of trains arriving at Magic Mall and standing there for less than 6 minutes before leaving is

    (A) none
    (B) 2
    (C) 7
    (D) 9

22. The number of trains shown on the schedule having different train numbers is

    (A) 6
    (B) 7
    (C) 8
    (D) 9

23. Going towards Harvard Square, Train #71 is scheduled to leave Pleasure Plaza at

    (A) 8:03
    (B) 8:18
    (C) 8:27
    (D) 8:30

24. Passengers boarding at Harding Street and wishing to get to Harvard Square by 8:45 would have to board a train which is scheduled to leave Magic Mall no later than

    (A) 8:26
    (B) 8:30
    (C) 8:34
    (D) 8:38

25. Train #73 should leave Harding Street on its eastbound trip

    (A) 7 minutes after leaving Harvard Square
    (B) 8 minutes after leaving Harvard Square
    (C) 9 minutes after leaving Harvard Square
    (D) 10 minutes after leaving Harvard Square

26. Due to door trouble, Train #72 (Eastbound) is turned at Harding Street when it was scheduled to leave and this operation takes 5 minutes. Since the running time for the return trip back to Harvard Square is the same time as that for the Eastbound trip, it should arrive back at Harvard Square at

    (A) 8:22
    (B) 8:27
    (C) 8:31
    (D) 8:39

27. If a train comes to a sudden stop and there is a delay in proceeding, the conductor should explain the reason for the delay to the passengers in order to

    (A) prevent them from blaming the train crew
    (B) prevent them from going on the track
    (C) keep them informed and calm
    (D) get them to help each other

28. Recently, the NYCTA instituted a program of closing off the rear portion of subway trains between the hours of 8 P.M. and 4 A.M. This was done mainly to

    (A) ease the job of the conductor
    (B) cut down on the number of people needed to operate trains
    (C) allow necessary repairs to be made in the closed off cars
    (D) attempt to cut down on crime in the subways

Questions 29 through 33 are based on the Broad Street Line timetable printed below. The numbers represent the *total* time (in minutes) that it takes the Broad Street Line local and express trains to travel from Frankford Avenue to the stations listed. The running times shown on the table include station-stop times. When answering these questions, use this timetable.

Broad Street Line

Stations	Total Running Times, in Minutes	
	Local	Express
Frankford Avenue	—	—
Columbus Street	7	—
Overland Parkway	12½	10
Victoria Boulevard	15	—
Market Street	17	14
Prince Street	24	—
Kings Avenue	28	—
Elizabeth Drive	33	28
Paradox Place	35	—
Del Prado Parkway	38½	33
Monroe Avenue	44	—
McKinley Plaza	48	41

29. Both an express train and local train are standing in the Market Street Station. If both trains leave Market Street at the same time, how many minutes would a rider save by using an express train in traveling to Del Prado Parkway?

(A) 1½ minutes
(B) 2½ minutes
✓(C) 3½ minutes
(D) 4½ minutes

30. If a Broad Street Local train leaves Columbus Street at 8:10 P.M., it should arrive at Monroe Avenue at

(A) 8:22 P.M.
(B) 8:34 P.M.
(C) 8:41 P.M.
(D) 8:47 P.M.

31. A passenger takes a local train from Columbus Street to Overland Parkway and then an express train from Overland Parkway to McKinley Plaza. Assuming no waiting time at any station, the total trip should take

(A) 36½ minutes
(B) 43½ minutes
(C) 46½ minutes
(D) 51½ minutes

32. A Broad Street Local leaves Frankford Avenue at 9:15 A.M. A Broad Street Express leaves Frankford Avenue at 9:18 A.M. At what station will the express meet the local?

(A) Overland Parkway
(B) Market Street
(C) Elizabeth Drive
(D) Del Prado Parkway

33. A conductor on the Broad Street Line is scheduled to make three round trips on the local train between Frankford Avenue and McKinley Plaza with a 6 minute layover at these two terminal stations. What is the total running time including time for layovers?

(A) 4 hours and 30 minutes
(B) 4 hours and 36 minutes
(C) 5 hours and 18 minutes
(D) 5 hours and 24 minutes

34. A passenger complains to a conductor that a public telephone in the station is not working and that she lost 25 cents in trying to use it. The conductor should tell her to

    (A) contact the Telephone Subdivision of the Maintenance of Way Department
    (B) complain to the railroad clerk on duty in the change booth
    (C) contact the NY Telephone Company for a refund
    (D) make a complaint to a transit patrolman

35. If a conductor reads a bulletin which he doesn't understand, the best thing for him to do is to

    (A) try to follow the directions in the bulletin as well as he can
    (B) discuss the bulletin with other conductors
    (C) ask the motorman of his train for an explanation
    (D) ask his supervisor what the bulletin means

36. A person has fallen on the subway station platform and says he has broken his leg. While waiting for an ambulance, a conductor should

    (A) help him over to a bench while putting as little weight as possible on the injured leg
    (B) make him as comfortable as possible without moving him
    (C) examine him for other possible injuries
    (D) apply a tourniquet to his leg from a first aid kit

37. Smoking in subway cars in prohibited mainly because it can

    (A) endanger a smoker's health
    (B) cause fires
    (C) bother passengers
    (D) cause cars to be littered with cigarette butts

38. Making an emergency stop of a subway train should be avoided, if possible, mainly because it might cause

    (A) passengers to be late for work
    (B) a train derailment
    (C) hard wear on brakes and rails
    (D) injuries to passengers

39. A passenger who seems to be drunk but has not disturbed anyone sits down on a seat near the conductor's cab. Of the following, the best way for the conductor to handle this situation is to

    (A) gently lead this passenger off the train at the next station
    (B) pay no attention to this passenger
    (C) contact the transit police and ask them to remove this passenger
    (D) do nothing but check frequently to see if this passenger starts to annoy anyone

40. Of the following, the best way for a conductor to keep informed of the latest changes in work procedures is to

    (A) read all the new bulletins when he signs in
    (B) study the book of rules
    (C) ask the other conductors
    (D) depend on his supervisor to tell him

41. A conductor has just finished her tour of duty. As she is leaving the terminal she finds a portion of the station platform has become slippery as a result of an oil spill. Which of the following is the best action for the conductor to take?

    (A) Write a report to her supervisor about the condition of the platform.
    (B) Warn any other employees that she sees before leaving about the condition of the platform.
    (C) Report the condition of the platform to her supervisor when she sees him.
    (D) Contact her supervisor about the condition of the platform before leaving the station.

42. While you are working as a conductor on a train, a friend of yours boards the train and tries to engage you in a long conversation. You should

    (A) continue the conversation only between stations
    (B) suggest that your friend talk to you only in the conductor's cab
    (C) tell your friend that private conversations are not allowed while you are working
    (D) request your friend to go into another car

43. The maximum number of cars which can be used on a subway train depends mainly on the

    (A) length of station platforms in the subway system
    (B) number of drive motors in each subway car
    (C) headway between trains during rush-hours
    (D) number of matched pairs of new-type subway cars making up the train

44. If a conductor in a station sees an armed robber "mugging" a passenger, he should

    (A) run up to the street and look for help
    (B) look for a weapon to attack the robber
    (C) call on other passengers to help him catch the robber
    (D) quickly contact the nearest transit police officer

86 / Bus Operator

Questions 45 through 55 are based on the map of imaginary rapid transit railroad systems shown on page 87. Consult this map when answering these questions.

45. The lines generally traveling east-west are

(A) Valley Road and Broad Boulevard
(B) Center Street and Hillside Avenue
(C) Cross Street Shuttle and Center Street
(D) Middle Street and Bridge Route

46. Of the three transfer points on the Broad Boulevard Line,

(A) two are to other systems and one to its own system
(B) all are to other systems
(C) all are to its own system
(D) one is to another system and two to its own system.

47. The express stations between which there is the greatest number of local stops are the

(A) South 12 Street and North 35 Street stations
(B) South 12 Street and Center Street stations
(C) Middle Street and South 34 Street stations
(D) Hill Road and Middle Street stations

48. A route traveled by more than one system is

(A) jointly operated by the CTS and the XBS systems
(B) jointly operated by the Bridge and the XBS systems
(C) jointly operated by the Bridge and the CTS systems
(D) not indicated on the map

49. The largest number of express stations on any one line is

(A) 3
(B) 6
(C) 7
(D) 9

50. If free transfers between different *systems* were issued only at adjacent express stops, the total possible number of such free transfer points is

(A) 1
(B) 2
(C) 3
(D) 0

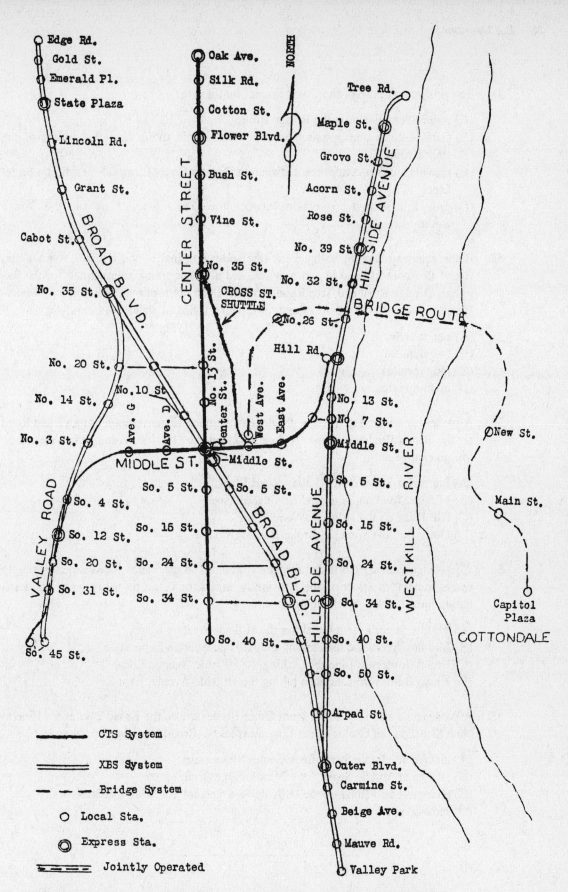

51. The primary purpose of the Cross Street Shuttle is to

    (A) reduce congestion on the Bridge Route
    (B) provide more transportation facilities for people living near the middle of the shuttle route
    (C) provide a direct connection between the Center Street Line and the Middle Street Line
    (D) provide a second connection between the Center Street Line and the Bridge Route

52. If the headway leaving Valley Park (the south terminal of the Hillside Avenue and Broad Boulevard Lines) is two minutes, and alternate trains are destined for the terminals at Edge Road and Tree Road respectively, a platformman at South 34th Street-Hillside Avenue Line would expect northbound trains to arrive at intervals of

    (A) one minute
    (B) two minutes
    (C) four minutes
    (D) eight minutes

53. A passenger wishing to travel with the least number of train changes from Edge Road on the Broad Boulevard Line to Tree Road on the Hillside Avenue Line should be told to change at

    (A) South 4th Street on the Valley Road Line
    (B) Middle Street on the Broad Boulevard Line
    (C) Hill Road on the Hillside Avenue Line
    (D) Outer Boulevard on the Broad Boulevard Line

54. A passenger leaving North 3rd Street southbound on the Valley Road Line wishing to reach South 15th Street on the Hillside Avenue Line could probably reach his destination most quickly by changing for the

    (A) Middle Street Line then taking the Hillside Avenue Local
    (B) Middle Street Line then taking the Hillside Avenue Express
    (C) Broad Boulevard Line then taking the Hillside Avenue Local
    (D) Broad Boulevard Line then taking the Hillside Avenue Express

55. A passenger wishing to travel from Outer Boulevard on the Broad Boulevard Line to Vine Street on the Center Street Line must take a Broad Boulevard train and

    (A) change at Middle Street for a Center Street train
    (B) change at Middle Street for a Middle Street train
    (C) change at Hill Road on the Hillside Avenue Line for a Middle Street train
    (D) remain on it

56. While a train is in passenger service, the conductor would be *least* concerned with the train's

    (A) heating
    (B) lighting
    (C) seating
    (D) ventilation

57. The basic reason why unauthorized persons must be prevented from entering on the tracks is that this practice is

    (A) dangerous
    (B) objectionable
    (C) prohibited
    (D) unlawful

58. Conductors must keep passageways on trains clear of obstructions to prevent

    (A) damage to property
    (B) injury to persons
    (C) complaints from passengers
    (D) possible fires

59. In cases where a disorderly person has to be ejected from New York City Transit System property, employees should first consider

    (A) the protection of transit property
    (B) maintenance of morale
    (C) the safety of passengers
    (D) their own safety

60. Disregarding rules relating to signals controlling train movements in the subway will

    (A) have no bearing on safety
    (B) greatly increase train speed
    (C) eliminate complaints from passengers
    (D) cause accidents

61. Subway accidents involving passengers occur most commonly on

    (A) the subway tracks
    (B) station stairways
    (C) station platforms
    (D) the street

62. A conductor should not open the side doors of a train until it has come to a full stop at a station because

    (A) she may be injured
    (B) the doors may be damaged
    (C) she would be reprimanded
    (D) a passenger might fall out

63. The north and south boundaries of Central Park are at

    (A) 59th & 110th Streets
    (B) 72nd & 116th Sreets
    (C) 63rd & 110th Streets
    (D) 57th & 116th Streets

64. Employees crossing from one platform to the other at stations should do so by way of

    (A) tracks
    (B) street
    (C) mezzanine or underpass
    (D) any one of these ways

65. The most important duty of a conductor assigned to platform work is

    (A) to see that exit facilities are so arranged as to permit passengers to exit or to permit authorized persons to enter
    (B) to render assistance needed to maintain scheduled movement of trains
    (C) to see that entry and departure through exit gates is made in an orderly manner
    (D) to watch all turnstiles

66. If the track becomes flooded due to a broken water main, a train should

    (A) be operated by power through the flooded section
    (B) be operated by coasting through the flooded section
    (C) not attempt to pass through the flooded area without obtaining permission from someone in competent authority
    (D) be brought to a stop and nearest emergency alarm box lever operated

67. Of the following, the best way to treat a person suffering from shock is to

    (A) lay the patient on back, head low, and loosen clothing around neck, chest, and abdomen
    (B) seat patient and keep warm with blankets
    (C) lay patient on stomach, head up, and loosen clothing
    (D) lay patient on back and massage about head, chest, and abdomen

68. If while working as a platform conductor you observe a person acting suspiciously and you believe he is going to commit suicide, you should

    (A) talk to the person and escort him to the street
    (B) have an agent call police and detain the person until an officer arrives to question him and take control
    (C) immediately obtain his name and address and arrange for a taxi to take him home
    (D) disregard the person entirely and allow him to go his own way

69. To properly protect the safety of passengers, property, and employees, it is essential that a conductor

    (A) obey all rules
    (B) be courteous
    (C) be brave
    (D) maintain self control

70. While you are on platform duty, a passenger is injured at your station. Upon inquiry as to how the accident occurred, she states, "It is not worth reporting." You should

    (A) do nothing further as apparently the passenger is not seriously injured
    (B) obtain her name and address and file them away in case further information is wanted at a future date
    (C) submit a report on the prescribed form
    (D) write a report stating that you rendered all practical assistance

71. The Museum of the City of New York is located at

    (A) 81st Street and Central Park West
    (B) 103rd Street and Fifth Avenue
    (C) 66th Street and Fifth Avenue
    (D) 99th Street and Central Park West

72. The Brooklyn Museum is located at

    (A) Flatbush Avenue and Linden Boulevard
    (B) Court and Fulton Streets
    (C) Atlantic and Nostrand Avenues
    (D) Eastern Parkway and Washington Avenue

73. The tallest building in New York City is the

    (A) Woolworth Building
    (B) Empire State Building
    (C) World Trade Center
    (D) Sears Tower

74. The New York Botanical Garden is located in

    (A) Central Park
    (B) Bronx Park
    (C) Prospect Park
    (D) Clove Lakes Park

75. The final signal which a conductor gives to the motorman that it is safe to proceed is the

    (A) air gage lighted on motorman's cab
    (B) hand signal
    (C) "all aboard" voice signal
    (D) buzzer signal

76. If a passenger approaches you with a package of cigarettes in his hand while you are on duty and asks you for a match, you should

    (A) tell him, in a polite manner, that you do not have a match
    (B) give him a match
    (C) tell him it is against the law to smoke in the subway
    (D) refer him to the station agent

77. When passengers appear unable to take care of themselves by reason of intoxication or apparent illness, the conductor must

    (A) immediately call a police officer
    (B) eject the offenders using such force as is necessary
    (C) escort them to the street
    (D) detain them until police patrol arrives and have them arrested

78. Brighton Beach is located in the county of

    (A) Kings
    (B) Queens
    (C) Richmond
    (D) New York

79. Of the following buildings, the one closest to Grand Central Terminal is the

    (A) Times Building
    (B) Flatiron Building
    (C) Empire State Building
    (D) Chrysler Building

80. Bellevue Hospital is located at

    (A) 1st Avenue and East 26th Street
    (B) 29th Street and 10th Avenue
    (C) 33rd Street and First Avenue
    (D) 14th Street and First Avenue

FOURTH SAMPLE EXAM

Bus Operator / Conductor

DIRECTIONS: Choose the best answer to each question and mark its letter, (A), (B), (C), or (D), on your answer sheet.

1. A driver should *not* permit his engine to run for long in an enclosed area mainly because gasoline engine exhaust is

    (A) irritating
    (B) explosive
    (C) corrosive
    (D) poisonous

2. Sudden stopping of a bus is to be avoided mainly because

    (A) some injury to passengers may result
    (B) some damage to the bus may result
    (C) this might tie up traffic
    (D) this might cause a skid

3. A bus operator, making his last run for the day, notices that the reading of the engine oil pressure gage has dropped to zero when he is about 20 blocks from the end of the run. He would do best to

    (A) complete the run and let the next operator report it
    (B) stop and make the necessary repairs
    (C) complete the run and report the condition on arrival
    (D) stop the bus and telephone headquarters

4. When initially warming up a bus diesel engine which is cold, the engine should be

    (A) raced violently
    (B) run at slightly above idling speed
    (C) raced rapidly in intermittent spurts
    (D) run fast enough to keep engine oil pressure at maximum indication

5. With respect to bus operation in heavy traffic, it is correct to state that

   (A) a bus operator could make better progress if most passenger car operators were not such poor drivers
   (B) a bus should have right of way over a passenger car because the bus carries more persons
   (C) a bus operator should not take advantage of the size of his vehicle
   (D) the bus operator is helping to speed up traffic when he pumps the brake pedal making frequent sounds of air release

6. Bus operators are warned to be careful when operating on rough sections of road, and to particularly avoid striking holes in the roadway. This care is necessary in order to avoid

   (A) the excessive noise
   (B) further damage to the roadway
   (C) damage to the bus
   (D) possible injury to adjacent cars

7. In preparing to make a right turn, it is *not* necessary for you to

   (A) move to the extreme right hand lane
   (B) slow down
   (C) give a hand or mechanical turn signal
   (D) come to a full stop

8. The right of way, in proceeding across an intersection against a red light, is *not* given to

   (A) a private passenger car taking a patient from a hospital
   (B) a fire engine truck returning to the fire house after a fire
   (C) a vehicle instructed to pass the red light by the traffic officer on duty at the intersection
   (D) a pedestrian guided by a seeing-eye dog

9. The driver of a truck cuts over in front of a bus, blocking further movement of the bus. He gets out of his truck and complains violently to the bus operator that the bus cut him off some distance back, forcing him to stop suddenly to avoid a collision with the bus. In this case, it would be best for the bus operator to

   (A) cut the argument short by moving the obstructing truck out of the way
   (B) avoid argument by saying it was unavoidable if it occurred and request the truck driver to move his truck
   (C) send a passenger to look for a traffic officer
   (D) request the passengers to verify the fact that the bus driver was not guilty of this accusation

10. A rule of the New York City Transit Authority is that operators of buses must never accept cash fares by hand, but must request passengers to deposit their own fares in the fare-box. The most likely reason for this rule is to

    (A) reduce the chance of money dropping to the floor of the bus
    (B) register every fare through the box
    (C) permit the passenger to count his change
    (D) prevent distraction of the operator while he is driving the bus

11. Of the following New York City parks, the one which is located in the Borough of Queens is

    (A) Flushing Meadow
    (B) Van Cortlandt
    (C) Prospect
    (D) Pelham Bay

12. Washington Square Park is located in

    (A) Brooklyn
    (B) Queens
    (C) the Bronx
    (D) Manhattan

13. Of the following places of interest, the one which is *not* a government building is

    (A) City Hall
    (B) the Criminal Courts Building
    (C) the Municipal Building
    (D) Grand Central Station

14. All questions on the standard motor vehicle accident report forms should be answered as fully as possible because

    (A) otherwise the report will be returned
    (B) it is easier to properly place responsibility
    (C) any further investigation is made unnecessary
    (D) short answers are bound to be incomplete

15. As the bus is about to come to a normal stop, the brakes are usually partially released in order to

    (A) make a smoother stop
    (B) be ready to start quicker after the stop
    (C) call the stop to the attention of the passengers by the sound of the air release
    (D) operate the doors

16. After a bus whose destination is Coney Island has traveled about half its route, a passenger boarding the bus at a stop asks, "Does this bus go to Coney Island?" The operator should

(A) ask the passenger to read the sign on the front
(B) explain to the passenger that all buses on the route go there
(C) simply tell the passenger "Yes" and check the destination sign if there is any doubt of its position
(D) say nothing but point to the side destination sign

17. In operating a car or bus over a slippery stretch of road between stops, it is best to

(A) keep the hand brake on lightly
(B) keep a small amount of power applied to the wheels
(C) coast
(D) alternately press and release the accelerator

Items 18 to 24 inclusive are based on the Extract of Rules for System Pick for Surface Line Operators given below. Read this extract carefully before answering these items.

EXTRACT OF RULES FOR SYSTEM PICK FOR SURFACE LINE OPERATORS

Operators picking an early run (one ending before 9:00 P.M. including all time allowances) on weekdays must pick an early run on Saturday and Sunday.

No operator will be allowed to pick on the extra list unless he desires to transfer to a depot where all runs, tricks, etc., have been picked.

After an operator finishes picking and the monitor has entered the operator's name for the run on the picking board, no change of run will be permitted. Erasures and other signs of mutilation will not be permitted on the picking board.

It is planned to permit about 100 operators in the picking room at one time, but the time allowed for any one person to pick will not exceed five minutes. If for any reason you cannot attend, you may submit a preference slip or be represented by proxy.

An operator inactive because of sickness, injury, etc., for sixty days prior to his pick assignment must present a certificate from a doctor stating he or she may return to duty not later than two weeks after date of pick.

Your cooperation is requested. Please be on hand to pick at your designated time and leave the picking room promptly when you have finished picking.

18. The rules apply to a

    (A) Saturday and Sunday pick
    (B) depot extra pick
    (C) weekday pick
    (D) system pick

19. An operator picking an early run on weekdays

    (A) cannot be off on Saturdays or Sundays
    (B) must submit a preference slip
    (C) will be assigned to the extra list on other days
    (D) must pick an early run on Saturday and Sunday

20. According to these rules, an operator

    (A) will be in the picking room alone while designating his choice
    (B) must wait in the picking room after making his choice until all the runs have been chosen
    (C) is informed that he may pick his run at any time he wishes to on pick day
    (D) may have someone else pick for him if he cannot be present on the day of the pick

21. In order to pick on the extra list, an operator must

    (A) present a doctor's certificate
    (B) have been inactive for sixty days
    (C) appear at the picking room in person
    (D) be willing to transfer to a terminal where all the runs have been picked

22. Once a bus operator picks a run and his name has been entered by the monitor he

    (A) must accept the run picked as no changes will be permitted
    (B) can change his mind if the choice was made by proxy
    (C) may ask the monitor to erase his pick if the next man has not yet picked
    (D) can swap runs with another operator but only after sixty days

23. An operator making his pick after having been out sick for three months must

    (A) pick on the extra list
    (B) present a doctor's certificate to the monitor
    (C) wait two weeks before returning to duty
    (D) pick an early run or trick

24. The rules state that

    (A) only 100 operators can pick in any one day
    (B) cooperation is demanded and a penalty will be imposed on any operator who is uncooperative
    (C) a preference slip must be signed by the monitor
    (D) an operator must make his pick within 5 minutes' time

---

25. An employee of the Transit Authority must notify the office whenever he moves and changes his address. The logical reason for this requirement is to

    (A) enable the authority to furnish correct information to creditors
    (B) enable the authority to contact the employee in time of need
    (C) prevent the holding of two jobs
    (D) help the post office, if necessary

26. The trend in New York City is changing all north and south avenues in Manhattan to one-way traffic. An important reason for this change is that

    (A) curb parking space is greatly increased
    (B) pedestrians have more opportunities to cross the avenues
    (C) traffic can move along the avenues with fewer delays
    (D) noise is reduced

27. Some bus operators work "swing tricks"; that is, they work about four hours, are off for two hours, and then work for another four hours. They are paid only for the time they work. The logical reason for having such split tours of work is that these operators

    (A) are assigned to work on two widely separated bus lines
    (B) have physical disabilities and cannot work a straight 8-hour tour
    (C) are needed only to man the extra rush-hour buses
    (D) handle the older buses which must be repaired during the day

28. Although lateness of any transit employee is undesirable, it is plain that a bus operator must make a special effort to report to work on time mainly because

    (A) he might be delayed by traffic
    (B) his bus must be warmed up before leaving the garage
    (C) lateness is always an indication of operator carelessness
    (D) bus schedules cannot be maintained otherwise

29. Subway maps do not give information about the

    (A) waiting time between trains
    (B) location of transfer points
    (C) terminals of the various lines
    (D) relative positions of express stations

30. The Transit Authority permits the posting of advertisements in buses

    (A) for the convenience of passengers
    (B) to increase income
    (C) because it permits subway advertising
    (D) to encourage bus riding

31. A passenger using crutches is boarding a crowded bus with difficulty. The operator should

    (A) request the passenger's crutches and store them behind the operator's seat
    (B) request that a suitable passenger near the door give up his or her seat
    (C) request the disabled passenger to wait for a less crowded bus
    (D) drive slowly until someone has given the disabled passenger a seat

32. A person who is obviously under the influence of liquor boards a bus. The operator should

    (A) order him off the bus promptly
    (B) let him remain on if he pays his fare, but watch his actions from time to time
    (C) use the horn to signal the nearest police officer for assistance
    (D) put him in charge of another passenger

33. An angry passenger getting off a bus at the front door loudly blames the operator for not stopping at the preceding bus stop. If the operator knows that the stop signal was not given until the bus was actually passing the preceding stop, his best course is to

    (A) say he didn't hear the signal
    (B) tell the passenger to complain to the management
    (C) ask other passengers to be his witness
    (D) say nothing and continue normal operation

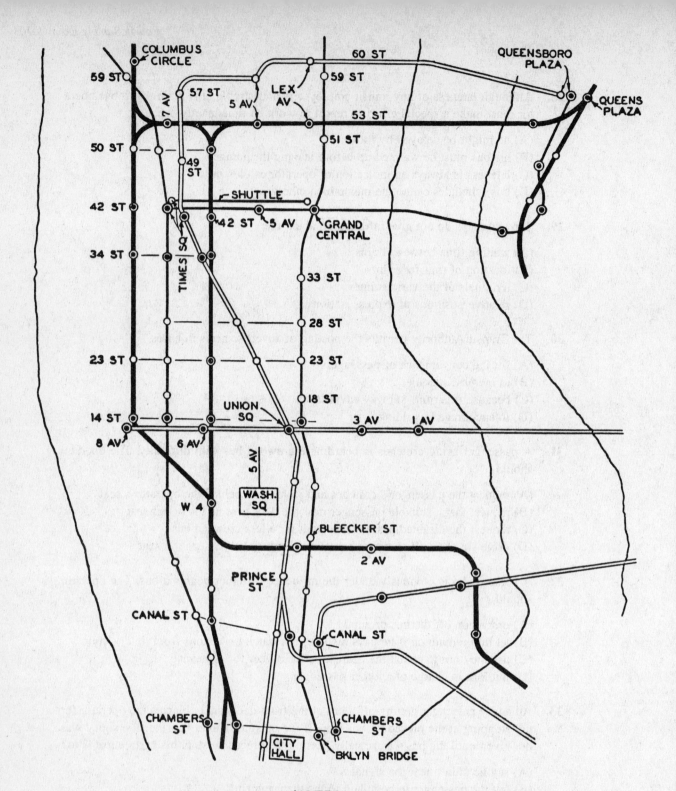

When answering Items 34 to 42 inclusive, refer to the map on page 104 as a guide.

34. In going from Queens Plaza or Queensboro Plaza to City Hall by express train, the fewest number of station stops will be made if a passenger takes the

    (A) IND and changes at West 4th Street
    (B) IRT and changes at Grand Central
    (C) IRT and changes at Times Square
    (D) BMT and changes at 14th Street

35. The subway lines which stop closest to the Pennsylvania Railroad Station are the

    (A) IRT—Bway-7th Avenue line; and the IND—8th Avenue line
    (B) IRT—Lexington Avenue line; and the BMT line
    (C) IND—8th Avenue line; and the IND—6th Avenue line
    (D) IND—6th Avenue line; and the BMT line

36. The most direct way to go from Times Square to 14th Street and 1st Avenue, by express trains, is to take

    (A) the BMT to Union Square and change to another BMT for 1st Avenue
    (B) the IRT to 14th Street and change to the BMT for 1st Avenue
    (C) the IND (6th Avenue) to 14th Street, and change to the BMT for 1st Avenue
    (D) the IND (8th Avenue) to 14th Street, and change to the BMT for 1st Avenue

37. The simplest way to go from Queensboro Plaza to Central Park is by way of the

    (A) BMT to the 5th Avenue Station
    (B) IND to the 5th Avenue Station
    (C) IRT to the Columbus Circle Station
    (D) IND to the Columbus Circle Station

38. On the BMT, between the Lexington Avenue station and the 14th Street station, the map shows

    (A) 5 express and no local stations
    (B) 1 express and 5 local stations
    (C) 2 express and 6 local stations
    (D) 2 express and 5 local stations

39. The express station nearest to the Public Library at 5th Avenue and 42nd Street is the

    (A) IRT—5th Avenue Station
    (B) BMT—Times Square Station
    (C) Grand Central Station on the shuttle
    (D) IND—5th Avenue Station

40. Between 42nd Street and Chambers Street the fewest number of station stops is made by an express train on the

    (A) BMT line
    (B) IRT Lexington Avenue line
    (C) IND—6th Avenue line
    (D) IRT—Broadway-7th Avenue line

41. A passenger coming to Manhattan on the 14th Street-Canarsie line and intending to go north to 42nd Street can do so without paying another fare by changing to a north-bound train at the

    (A) 6th Avenue, 8th Avenue or Union Square stations
    (B) 7th Avenue station
    (C) 8th Avenue station
    (D) Union Square station

42. Between 45th Street and 63rd Street in Manhattan the map shows a total of

    (A) 5 express and 9 local stations
    (B) 9 express and 5 local stations
    (C) 5 express and 8 local stations
    (D) 8 express and 5 local stations

---

43. When a certain bus stops for a red traffic light at a busy mid-town intersection (not a bus stop), a passenger pulls the stop cord several times and loudly demands to be let off. The wisest course for the operator is to

    (A) open the door promptly to avoid further commotion
    (B) warn the passenger to stop making a nuisance of himself
    (C) tell the passenger it is against the law to let him off there
    (D) inch the bus along to keep the passenger off balance until the light changes

44. Although a bus operator has continually requested the passengers to "move to the rear, please," the passengers continue to obstruct the entrance door even though there is considerable room in the rear. The *least* effective further action would be for the operator to

    (A) refuse to move the bus until the passengers do move
    (B) stand up, turn around, and directly address the particular people who are not moving
    (C) alternately brake and accelerate the bus
    (D) make the request "Please cooperate, others want to get to work too."

45. If the bus stop signal used by passengers becomes inoperative on a crowded bus about halfway between terminals, the procedure likely to cause the least confusion is for the operator to

    (A) continue in passenger service requesting passengers to call out their stops
    (B) accept no more passengers but continue to make regular stops to discharge the passengers already on the bus
    (C) stop and transfer all passengers to following buses
    (D) locate the trouble and fix it

46. It is correct to state that the greater the speed of a vehicle,

    (A) the easier it is to stop
    (B) the easier it is to turn a corner
    (C) the longer the tire life
    (D) the harder it is to control the vehicle

47. If a vehicle swerves to one side whenever a sudden stop is made, the most likely cause is

    (A) a defective transmission
    (B) a defective rear axle
    (C) uneven brakes
    (D) uneven steering radius

48. The very slow driver is considered a safety menace mainly because

    (A) he never knows where he is going
    (B) he is always driving a defective vehicle
    (C) other cars are constantly cutting out to pass him
    (D) he may back up at any moment

49. The safest procedure to follow when another car is attempting to pass you on the road is to

    (A) sound your horn
    (B) be prepared to slow down
    (C) speed up
    (D) pay no attention to him

50. The best procedure for a bus operator to follow, at an intersection where the traffic lights are stuck in the red position for all traffic, is to

    (A) wait for a traffic officer
    (B) proceed cautiously across the intersection when traffic permits
    (C) wait for a signal maintenance man
    (D) have a passenger stop opposing traffic so you can cross

51. Night driving is more dangerous than daytime driving mainly because

    (A) road vision is reduced
    (B) more drivers ignore the traffic lights
    (C) more people are shopping
    (D) there are fewer police cars on duty

Items 52 to 60 inclusive are based on the bus timetable shown on page 109. Assume layover time at Prince Street and Duke Street is negligible. Refer to this timetable when answering these items.

52. The total *running* time (omit layover) for one round trip from King Street to Queen Street and back again is

(A) 70 minutes
(B) 65 minutes
(C) 60 minutes
(D) 30 minutes

53. The *least* time that any bus stops over at Queen Street is

(A) 3 minutes
(B) 5 minutes
(C) 10 minutes
(D) 15 minutes

54. The time required for a bus to make the Eastbound run from King Street to Queen Street is

(A) 65 minutes
(B) 60 minutes
(C) 35 minutes
(D) 30 minutes

55. The total number of different buses shown in the timetable is

(A) 8
(B) 9
(C) 10
(D) 12

56. The timetable shows that the total number of buses which make two round trips is

(A) 1
(B) 2
(C) 3
(D) 4

57. A person reaching Duke Street at 8:28 to leave on a Westbound bus will have to wait

(A) 2 minutes
(B) 5 minutes
(C) 7 minutes
(D) 10 minutes

58. The shortest *running* time between any two bus stops is

(A) 3 minutes
(B) 5 minutes
(C) 10 minutes
(D) 15 minutes

Bus No.	EASTBOUND					WESTBOUND		
	King St. Leave	Prince St. Leave	Duke St. Leave	Queen St. Arrive	Queen St. Leave	Duke St. Leave	Prince St. Leave	King St. Arrive
20	7:15	7:20	7:30	7:45	7:50	8:05	8:15	8:20
21	7:25	7:30	7:40	7:55	8:00	8:15	8:25	8:30
22	7:35	7:40	7:50	8:05	8:10	8:25	8:35	8:40
23	7:45	7:50	8:00	8:15	8:20	8:35	8:45	8:50
24	7:55	8:00	8:10	8:25	8:30	8:45	8:55	9:00
25	8:05	8:10	8:20	8:35	8:40	8:55	9:05	9:10
26	8:10	8:15	8:25	8:40	8:43	8:58	9:08	9:13
27	8:15	8:20	8:30	8:45	8:48	9:03	9:13	9:18
28	8:20	8:25	8:35	8:50	8:53	9:08	9:18	9:23
20	8:30	8:35	8:45	9:00	9:05	9:20	9:30	9:35
21	8:40	8:45	8:55	9:10	9:15	9:30	9:40	9:45
22	8:50	8:55	9:05	9:20	9:25	9:40	9:50	9:55

59. The bus which arrives at King Street three minutes after the preceding bus is bus

(A) No. 20
(B) No. 22
(C) No. 26
(D) No. 28

60. Bus No. 21 is scheduled to start its second round trip from King Street at

(A) 9:45
(B) 8:40
(C) 8:30
(D) 7:25

61. The Sunday timetable is generally operated in place of the regular weekday timetable when a legal holiday falls on a weekday. The logical reason is that passenger travel

    (A) is never heavy on a holiday
    (B) is heaviest on Sundays and holidays
    (C) on weekdays is heavier than on holidays
    (D) on holidays is generally similar to Sunday travel

62. If one person threatens another with personal violence in the presence of an operator, the operator should

    (A) pay no attention to them for they are only talking
    (B) tell them if they don't stop making a disturbance in a public place, a special patrolman will be called
    (C) call for help
    (D) wait to see if the person actually carries out his threats

63. Courtesy to passengers is impressed on transit employees mainly to

    (A) discourage vandalism
    (B) assure passenger safety
    (C) speed up bus operations
    (D) maintain good public relations

64. It is reasonable to expect that a bus operator would be required to

    (A) make minor repairs to his engine
    (B) change a burned out headlight lamp
    (C) make written reports of his activities
    (D) detain disorderly people

65. The usual attitude of an operator toward the public should be

    (A) suspicious
    (B) helpful
    (C) hostile
    (D) commanding

66. Employees must know the rules and regulations governing their jobs to

    (A) please their supervisors
    (B) foresee emergencies
    (C) avoid accidents
    (D) perform their duties properly

67. Operators should be in position to open doors

    (A) at all times
    (B) before the bus stops
    (C) immediately after the bus has stopped
    (D) when the bus is operating through tunnels underneath a river

68. Doors of a bus should not be closed until

    (A) every person at the stop has boarded the bus
    (B) the bus has come to a full stop
    (C) you observe it is safe to do so
    (D) the bus begins to move

69. A door which slams shut too quickly should not be operated because it

    (A) might open accidentally
    (B) might result in injury to a passenger
    (C) does not give passengers time to board the bus
    (D) does not give passengers time to leave the bus

70. When a bus is stopped and the front doors cannot be opened, the operator should

    (A) shorten the time needed for the stop
    (B) open the emergency exit
    (C) open and close the defective door by hand
    (D) give passengers a chance to leave through the rear door

Items 71 to 75 inclusive are based on the section of the New York State Vehicle and Traffic Law given below. Read this section carefully before answering these items.

The driver of a vehicle overtaking or meeting a bus which has stopped for the purpose of receiving or discharging passengers shall bring his vehicle to a complete stop and keep it stationary until such bus shall resume motion, or until signalled by the driver to proceed, provided flashing red signal lights and signs designating the bus as a school bus are displayed on such bus as required by law. The driver of such school bus, when discharging pupils who must cross the highway or street, shall instruct such pupils to cross in front of the bus and the driver thereof shall keep such school bus halted with red signal lights flashing until such pupils have reached the opposite side of the highway or street.

71. Such a law is necessary principally because

    (A) school buses make frequent stops
    (B) the children must get to school on time
    (C) the actions of children are unpredictable
    (D) school buses often stop on curves

72. The operator of a car meeting a standing bus covered by this law may pass the bus if

    (A) no children are crossing the street
    (B) the bus operator signals him to pass
    (C) he can pass at least 6 feet away
    (D) the bus appears to be empty of children

73. It is easiest to recognize such a school bus, when approaching it, by the

    (A) children
    (B) color
    (C) flashing lights
    (D) signs

74. When children must cross the street to go home after leaving the bus, the operator is specifically required to instruct them to

    (A) cross in front of the bus
    (B) signal when they have reached the other side
    (C) look both ways before crossing
    (D) hurry to the other side

75. The operator of a private car would be acting in accordance with the law if he took the flashing red lights on the bus to have the same meaning as a

    (A) flashing red traffic signal
    (B) flashing light on an ambulance
    (C) flashing yellow traffic signal
    (D) flashing railroad crossing signal

FIFTH SAMPLE EXAM

Bus Operator / Conductor

DIRECTIONS: Choose the best answer to each question and mark its letter, (A), (B), (C), or (D), on your answer sheet.

1. Many collisions occur even at intersections that are governed by well-maintained traffic lights. The most helpful lesson to be learned from this statement is that traffic lights

    (A) are no substitute for an alert driver
    (B) are poorly designed
    (C) have doubtful value
    (D) are often out of order

2. Of the following, steering gear damage is most likely to result from

    (A) sudden stops
    (B) fast acceleration
    (C) excess lubrication
    (D) hitting curbs

3. At an intersection, the driver who has the preferred right of way is the one who is

    (A) making a left turn
    (B) making a right turn
    (C) proceeding straight ahead
    (D) making a U-turn

4. If a tire blows out, it is most important for the driver to

    (A) hold the steering wheel tightly
    (B) disengage the clutch immediately
    (C) shift to low gear
    (D) keep his foot on the gas

5. Driving through water puddles during a rainstorm should be avoided mainly because of the danger of

    (A) the wheels rusting
    (B) rotting the tires
    (C) hitting deep holes
    (D) splashing the headlights

6. Axle and spring damage is most likely to occur on a bus which is driven rapidly on a roadway which

    (A) has wet leaves
    (B) is oiled
    (C) is rutted with ice
    (D) is sanded

7. A bus operator should never shift gears while on a railroad crossing because it may cause engine

    (A) stalling
    (B) knocking
    (C) overheating
    (D) bearing failure

8. When the wheels of a bus are stuck in deep snow, the *worst* thing for the bus operator to do is to

    (A) back up
    (B) try second gear
    (C) accelerate rapidly
    (D) start slowly

9. If a bus operator must leave his bus parked on a hilly street he should park with

    (A) rear wheels at least 3 inches from the curb
    (B) front wheels parallel to the curb
    (C) all wheels a few inches away from the curb
    (D) front wheels cut into the curb

10. The majority of traffic accidents are most likely caused by

    (A) negligence
    (B) defective vehicles
    (C) roadway conditions
    (D) defective traffic lights

11. The most important reason for keeping traffic accident statistics is to

    (A) justify law enforcement
    (B) determine accident causes
    (C) reduce speeding
    (D) frighten pedestrians

Items 12 to 16 inclusive in Column I are names of well-known points of interest in Manhattan each of which is most nearly in one of the four directions listed in Column II from the intersection of 42nd Street and Fifth Ave. For each name in Column I, select the most appropriate direction from Column II.

	COLUMN I (names)	COLUMN II (directions)
ITEM		
12.	Empire State Building	(A) north
13.	United Nations Headquarters (Glass-faced building)	(B) east
		(C) south
14.	Times Square	
		(D) west
15.	Radio City	
16.	Washington Square	

17. Standard forms frequently call for entries on them to be printed. This is done mainly because printing, as compared to writing, is generally

    (A) more compact
    (B) more legal
    (C) more legible
    (D) easier to do

18. If an angry passenger, boarding a bus at a busy stop, called the operator names because the bus was late, the operator would show best judgment by

    (A) ignoring the name calling
    (B) explaining the reason for the lateness to the passenger
    (C) ejecting the passenger
    (D) getting the passenger's name and address

19. An operator becomes aware that several boys are "hitching" a ride on the outside of his bus. It would probably be best for the operator to

    (A) ignore them
    (B) ask the passengers to scare them off
    (C) try to shake them off by "jerking" the bus along
    (D) order them to get off, but take no other direct action until he reaches a supervisor or patrolman

20. When operating your bus, you hear a siren from behind on an overtaking vehicle. The best of the following actions for you to take is to

    (A) pull over to the right as far as possible and stop
    (B) speed up
    (C) stop wherever you are and let the vehicle pass
    (D) continue normally except slow down

21. The operator is forbidden by the rules to converse unnecessarily with passengers while driving his bus. A logical reason for this rule is that such conversation

    (A) takes the operator's attention off his driving
    (B) makes a poor impression on the other passengers
    (C) tends to block the entrance to the bus
    (D) may lead to an argument with undesirable consequences

Items 22 to 30 inclusive are based on the timetable given below. When answering these items refer to this timetable.

TRIP No.	TIMETABLE							
	EASTBOUND				WESTBOUND			
	RED TERMINAL	BLUE STATION	GREEN STATION	GRAY TERMINAL	GREEN STATION	BLUE STATION	RED TERMINAL	
	ARRIVES	LEAVES	LEAVES	LEAVES	ARRIVES	LEAVES	LEAVES	LEAVES	ARRIVES
1	11:51	12:00	12:14	12:29	12:45	12:53	1:09	1:24	1:38
2	12:03	12:20	12:34	12:49	1:05	1:13	1:29	1:44	1:58
3	12:30	12:40	12:54	1:09	1:25	1:33	1:49	2:04	2:18
4	12:45	1:00	1:14	1:29	1:45	1:53	2:09	2:24	2:38
5	1:00	1:20	1:34	1:49	2:05	2:13	2:29	2:44	2:58
6	1:18	1:40	1:54	2:09	2:25	2:33	2:49	3:04	3:18
7	1:38	2:00	2:14	2:29	2:45	2:53	3:09	3:24	3:38
8	1:58	2:20	2:34	2:49	3:05	3:13	3:29	3:44	3:58
9	2:18	2:40	2:54	3:09	3:25	3:33	3:49	4:04	4:18
10	2:38	3:00	3:14	3:29	3:45	3:53	4:09	4:24	4:38
11	2:58	3:20	3:34	3:49	4:05	4:13	4:29	4:44	4:58
12	3:18	3:40	3:54	4:09	4:25	4:33	4:49	5:04	5:18

Explanatory Note: Assume that train operations proceed without delay, unless otherwise stated.

22. If Trip No. 2 leaves the Gray Terminal 8 minutes late and loses an additional 4 minutes between each of the indicated stations or terminals, it will arrive at the Red terminal at

(A) 2:14
(B) 2:18
(C) 2:22
(D) 2:30

23. The number of trips leaving the Red Terminal between 1:35 and 2:35 is

(A) 3
(B) 4
(C) 8
(D) 9

24. The maximum number of trips leaving the Green Station in both eastbound and westbound directions in any 65 consecutive minutes is

(A) 3
(B) 4
(C) 6
(D) 8

25. The running time between the Red and Gray Terminals as scheduled for Trip No. 1 is

    (A) 45 minutes
    (B) 53 minutes
    (C) 1 hour 30 minutes
    (D) 1 hour 38 minutes

26. The total number of trips scheduled to be waiting at the terminals at 1:23 is

    (A) 1
    (B) 2
    (C) 3
    (D) 4

27. Trip No. 5 should leave the Blue Station on its westbound trip

    (A) 14 minutes after leaving the Red Terminal
    (B) 31 minutes after leaving the Red Terminal
    (C) 1 hour and 24 minutes after leaving the Red Terminal
    (D) 1 hour and 44 minutes after leaving the Red Terminal

28. Considering eastbound trips only, an error exists in the statement: Trip No. 4 is scheduled to arrive at the Gray Terminal

    (A) 4 minutes before Trip No. 5 leaves the Green Station
    (B) 5 minutes after Trip No. 6 leaves the Red Terminal
    (C) 16 minutes before Trip No. 4 leaves the Green Station
    (D) 9 minutes before Trip No. 6 leaves the Blue Station

29. The total number of trips scheduled to be in motion in a westbound direction at 2:10 is

    (A) 1
    (B) 2
    (C) 4
    (D) 5

30. Trip No. 9 is to be omitted and Trip No. 10 advanced to divide the interval between trips No. 8 and 11 evenly. Trip No. 10 would then be scheduled to leave the

    (A) Blue Station at 2:54
    (B) Green Station at 3:29
    (C) Gray Terminal at 3:35
    (D) Blue Station at 4:14

31. When driving a crowded bus, it may sometimes be preferable to have a minor collision rather than to brake to the most sudden stop possible. The principal reason is that

    (A) the bus may skid
    (B) buses are very heavily constructed against collision
    (C) a rear end collision may sometimes result
    (D) more persons may be injured by the sudden stop than the collision

32. If the operator of a bus hears two passengers arguing over the right to occupy a certain seat, it is best for the operator to

    (A) decide which passenger is entitled to the seat
    (B) ask both passengers to leave the bus
    (C) ignore the situation unless they resort to force
    (D) ask an impartial observer to settle the dispute

33. If traffic conditions permit, when passing a line of cars parked at the curb, the best driving procedure would be for the bus operator to drive the bus

    (A) about 3 feet away from the parked cars
    (B) within a few inches of the parked cars
    (C) at least a car width away from these cars
    (D) close to unoccupied cars and six feet away from occupied cars

34. If a bus operator is within a few bus stops from his terminal point, he would most likely have to request his passengers to take another bus if

    (A) the rear exit door should jam in the closed position
    (B) the rear exit door should jam in the open position
    (C) the fare box should become inoperative
    (D) the buzzer signal system goes out of order

35. If a passenger requests your badge number without any apparent reason, you should

    (A) ask him the reason for his request
    (B) refuse to give it to him
    (C) tell him to get the information from headquarters
    (D) give him your badge number without question

36. If two passengers ignore the bus operator's warning to stop vandalism while riding the bus, it would be best for the bus operator to

    (A) attract the attention of a police officer as soon as possible
    (B) ask the other passengers to leave the bus
    (C) forcibly eject the troublemakers
    (D) take the names and addresses of the troublemakers

Items 37 to 42 inclusive are based on the Information for Bus Operators given below. Read this information carefully before answering these items.

INFORMATION FOR BUS OPERATORS

In spite of caution signs and signal lights, more than 42% of all automobile accidents occur at intersections. In narrow city streets with narrow sidewalks and heavy traffic, you should approach intersections at 15 miles per hour with your foot just touching the brake pedal; in wet weather, 10 miles per hour. At rural intersections, be sure you have a clear view of the intersecting road to the right and left at least 300 feet before you reach the intersection, otherwise slow down.

At an intersection, the vehicle on your right has the right of way if both of you reach the intersection at the same time. You have the right of way over the vehicle at your left under the same condition, but must not insist upon it if there is risk of a collision.

Do not pass another vehicle at an intersection. Stop your vehicle to allow pedestrians to cross in front of you at intersections if they have stepped off the curb. Operators must use extreme caution when approaching or turning at intersections not controlled by a signal light.

37. One of the facts given is that

 (A) nearly all accidents occur at country crossroads
 (B) nearly half of all accidents occur at traffic lights in cities
 (C) approximately two-fifths of all accidents occur where roads or streets cross one another
 (D) 42% of all accidents occur on narrow city streets

38. According to this information, if you are approaching an intersection at which there is no traffic light, and a pedestrian has started to cross the street in front of you, you must

 (A) reduce your speed to 15 miles per hour
 (B) blow your horn lightly
 (C) stop to allow him to cross
 (D) place your foot so it just touches the brake pedal

39. At an intersection not protected by a traffic light, you should grant the right of way to the vehicle approaching from the

 (A) right if it is 300 feet from the intersection
 (B) left if it is 300 feet from the intersection
 (C) opposite direction if its right turn indicator is flashing
 (D) left or the right if there is danger of collision

40. In the information, it is clearly stated that an intersection should be approached at 15 miles per hour if you

 (A) are driving on a narrow city street in heavy traffic
 (B) do not see a warning sign 300 feet from the intersection
 (C) do not intend to pass the vehicle ahead
 (D) see a car stopped on the intersecting street waiting to cross

41. The information clearly states that

(A) most city streets are narrow
(B) all city intersections should be approached at 10 miles per hour
(C) passing another vehicle at an intersection is forbidden
(D) there is a clear view of rural intersections from a distance of 300 feet

42. The type of accident referred to probably does *not* include the striking of a

(A) pedestrian by a railroad train
(B) pedestrian by a passenger car
(C) bus by a taxicab
(D) bus by a truck

---

43. Before backing a bus, it is *most* important to

(A) give the proper hand signal
(B) blow your horn
(C) see that nothing is behind the bus
(D) turn on the back-up lights

44. The constant impact of passengers can be extremely wearing on the operator. Consequently, a new operator is well advised to

(A) discourage any passenger asking silly questions by the briefest possible reply
(B) remain cold and aloof from the passengers at all times
(C) remember the considerate passenger instead of dwelling on the faults of the relatively few
(D) view all passengers as a necessary evil

45. Your bus is being overtaken by a passenger car on a narrow two-way street. When the overtaking car is alongside your bus, its driver sees an oncoming car and starts to drop back. You can best help reduce the danger of accident to all three vehicles by

(A) pressing on the accelerator pedal
(B) slowing down and swinging to the right
(C) stepping on the brake pedal
(D) signaling the overtaking car to pass you

46. The midtown Port Authority Bus Terminal building is located at

(A) 40th Street and 8th Avenue
(B) 42nd Street and Broadway
(C) 50th Street and 6th Avenue
(D) 34th Street and 7th Avenue

47. A bus operator reports that while proceeding south on a certain street, the middle of the right side of his bus was hit by an eastbound truck which was making a left turn. It follows that the bus was struck by the

   (A) rear left corner of the truck
   (B) rear right corner of the truck
   (C) front left corner of the truck
   (D) front right corner of the truck

48. It is correct to say that the

   (A) Henry Hudson Bridge connects the Bronx and Queens
   (B) Holland Tunnel is under the East River
   (C) George Washington Bridge is near 59th Street
   (D) Brooklyn Bridge is near City Hall

49. On vehicles equipped with hydraulic braking, the most serious danger which may occur is

   (A) unequal braking
   (B) high brake fluid pressure
   (C) loss of the brake fluid
   (D) freezing of the brake fluid

50. On vehicles equipped with manual shifting, the practice of coasting out of gear is *undesirable* because

   (A) it wastes gas
   (B) the driver has less control of his vehicle
   (C) it causes engine damage
   (D) it generally causes rear axle damage

51. When passing a school, a bus operator's driving should be governed chiefly by the thought that

   (A) children are apt to run out on the street at any time
   (B) policemen at school crossings are apt to be hard on careless drivers
   (C) horns and bus engine noise distract children's attention from their class work
   (D) children may throw things at the bus

52. The best reason for a bus operator not to attempt to pass another moving bus on a grade is that

   (A) the strain on the engine may be too great
   (B) too much noise results
   (C) it may alarm the passengers
   (D) the slow operation will unduly delay other traffic

53. If a passenger urges a bus operator to travel as fast as possible because he is in a hurry to catch a train, the operator should

   (A) continue to operate normally
   (B) increase his speed between stops
   (C) skip a few stops
   (D) take a shorter alternate route

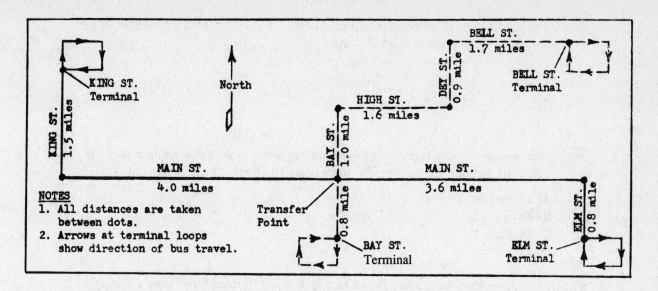

Items 54 to 61 inclusive are based on the above sketch showing the routes of the Main Street (solid line) and the Bay Street (dotted line) buses. Refer to this sketch when answering these items.

54. The distance from the King Street Terminal to the Elm Street Terminal is

    (A) 10 miles
    (B) 9.9 miles
    (C) 9.1 miles
    (D) 7.6 miles

55. A transfer is required for a passenger going from Bell Street Terminal to

    (A) Bay Street
    (B) Dey Street
    (C) High Street
    (D) Elm Street

56. A bus running on Main Street and going from Bay Street to Elm Street is moving

    (A) West
    (B) East
    (C) South
    (D) North

57. Buses are *not* required to make any left turn at

    (A) the King Street Terminal
    (B) the transfer point
    (C) the Bay Street Terminal
    (D) the Bell Street Terminal

128 / *Bus Operator*

58. After discharging all passengers at Bell Street Terminal, the number of right turns required for the bus to reach Bay Street is

    (A) 1
    (B) 2
    (C) 3
    (D) 4

59. If the average running speed of buses from King Street Terminal to the transfer point is 22 miles an hour, and the time for stops totals 10 minutes, then this trip takes

    (A) 25 minutes
    (B) 20 minutes
    (C) 15 minutes
    (D) 12 minutes

60. A bus going from Bay Street Terminal to Bell Street Terminal travels in a northerly direction a total distance of

    (A) 0.8 mile
    (B) 1.8 miles
    (C) 2.7 miles
    (D) 4.3 miles

61. The street having the shortest bus mileage is

    (A) Bay Street
    (B) Dey Street
    (C) Elm Street
    (D) King Street

62. It would be *least* desirable for a bus operator whose bus is in motion to tell a passenger

   (A) the location of a bus transfer point
   (B) the length of time required to reach his destination
   (C) to move away from the front doors
   (D) why his complaint of poor service is not justified

63. When driving up a hill on a narrow roadway, passing another car is dangerous because

   (A) it is difficult to make a quick stop
   (B) the engine will overheat
   (C) steering control is lost
   (D) vision is limited

64. Grease on brake lining

   (A) is necessary for long brake life
   (B) is necessary for quiet braking
   (C) results in unsafe brakes
   (D) results in safer braking

65. A bus operator is required to wear a prescribed standard uniform while on duty. The best reason for this requirement is that such a uniform

   (A) protects the operator's clothing
   (B) identifies the wearer as the official operator of the bus
   (C) is cheaper than ordinary clothing
   (D) gives the operator the greatest possible comfort

66. If a bus operator running his bus at 25 miles per hour notices that the reading of the engine oil pressure gauge has dropped to zero, he should

   (A) stop the bus
   (B) speed up to 30 miles per hour
   (C) drive at speeds below 20 miles per hour
   (D) shift to low gear

67. It would be correct to state that

   (A) it is impossible to slow down on ice
   (B) rain on a road increases traction
   (C) chains increase skidding in snow
   (D) most skids can be avoided

68. An operator entering a bus garage notices a lighting fixture that appears to be loose and in danger of falling from the ceiling. His best procedure would be to

(A) get a step ladder and tie the fixture up temporarily with cord
(B) find the switch and turn the light off
(C) tell his superior about the fixture
(D) forget it because the repairmen will find it

69. As a newly appointed bus operator, your supervisor would most likely expect you to

(A) pay close attention to instructions
(B) complete your runs ahead of schedule time
(C) make plenty of mistakes
(D) have arguments with passengers the first few days

70. At an intersection, having no traffic light or other protection, the right of way belongs to

(A) the avenue traffic
(B) pedestrians attempting to cross
(C) cars attempting to turn
(D) buses crossing the intersection to make a passenger stop

71. The traffic light blinker which warns a driver to cross an intersection with caution and be prepared to stop for cross traffic is a

(A) flashing yellow light
(B) green arrow below a red light
(C) flashing red light
(D) double red light

72. A flashing red traffic signal indicates that a driver

(A) may proceed past the signal cautiously without stopping
(B) must stop and then proceed when cross traffic allows
(C) must stop and wait until the light changes to flashing yellow
(D) must stop and wait until the light stops flashing

73. One of the rules governing the operators states that "They must not use buses to push other buses or vehicles unless ordered by a member of the supervisory force." According to this rule, if a taxicab driver asks the operator of an empty bus to give him a push to get started, the operator should

(A) tell the taxicab driver it is against the rules and go on
(B) do so if there is a patrolman nearby
(C) telephone headquarters to get permission
(D) tell the taxicab driver to ask the operator of a private car

74. A good bus operator best shows his skill by

   (A) never using his horn
   (B) driving with a minimum number of changes in speed between stops
   (C) stopping behind other cars with the smallest possible clearance
   (D) not reducing speed passing through narrow traffic openings

75. A driver should pay particular attention in making proper left turns because

   (A) more effort is required on the steering wheel
   (B) opposing traffic lanes must be crossed
   (C) it is more difficult to see pedestrians
   (D) they are sharper than right turns

76. If the temperature gage on a bus shows an excessively high temperature, it is usually caused by

   (A) too heavy a passenger load
   (B) too much braking
   (C) sustained high speed
   (D) an engine defect

77. Throgs Neck Bridge connects the Bronx and

   (A) Manhattan
   (B) Randall's Island
   (C) Brooklyn
   (D) Queens

78. Of the following New York City parks, the one which is located in the borough of Brooklyn is

   (A) Van Cortlandt
   (B) Jacob Riis
   (C) Great Kills
   (D) Prospect

79. In an effort to have a quieter city, a drive has been made during the past year against unnecessary use of automobile horns. A driver in this city is justified in using his horn when

   (A) another driver starts to get out on the traffic side of his parked car
   (B) a pedestrian crossing the street delays him in starting promptly on the green light
   (C) he wants to signal the car in front of him in the left-hand lane to move over to the right and permit him to pass
   (D) the car in front does not start off promptly as the traffic light changes to green

80. Some buses are equipped with three mirrors in the front: one outside the bus on the left, just forward of the operator's position; the second inside near the center, above the windshield; and the third inside in the upper right-hand corner above the front door. The purpose of the third mirror is to enable the operator to

(A) watch passengers using the rear door
(B) see how crowded the bus is
(C) watch entering passengers
(D) see traffic on the right side of the bus

On-Road Skills Test

Each person applying for a commercial driver's license must pass a special on-road skills test. This test checks to see if the driver can safely operate a commercial motor vehicle.

The examiner will instruct you over a preplanned road test route. The examiner will tell you to make turns, to back up, to stop, and to start throughout the route in order to evaluate your skills.

You must be able to correctly complete the following:
- Left turns
- Right turns
- A railroad crossing
- A stop and start on a grade
- Driving up a hill or grade
- Driving down a hill or grade
- Stopping at and going through intersections
- Driving on straight sections of urban/rural roads
- Driving around curves
- Driving under an underpass or across a bridge
- Driving on an expressway
- Backing in a straight line and parallel parking
- Forward stopping

Throughout the test, you will also be tested on your general driving skills:
- Using the clutch properly
- Using gears properly
- Using brakes properly
- Obeying traffic signs
- Operating the vehicle safely

The examiner will watch for certain actions as you go through the test. You should practice each of the test items to make sure you do them correctly. This section explains what the examiner will be checking.

As you approach each turn the examiner will check if you:
- Check traffic. You must look ahead, left, right, and to the rear using your mirrors.
- Signal. You must signal at least 100 feet before the turn.
- Slow down. Slow smoothly and change gears as needed to keep power. Do not coast with your foot on the clutch.
- Position your vehicle. Get into the correct lane and position your vehicle to make the turn.

You should time your arrival so stopping isn't necessary. If you must stop prior to the turn, the examiner will check if you:
- Maintain gap. Stop far enough back so you can see the rear wheels of the vehicle in front.
- Stop in correct place. Stop so your vehicle is not in the intersection, over the stop line, or past the sidewalk, stop sign, or other marker.
- Stop fully. You must not coast and must come to a full stop.
- Keep wheels straight. You must keep your wheels straight ahead while stopped.

While you are turning, the examiner will check if you:
- Check traffic.
- Keep both hands on the wheel.
- Change gears. You must not change gears during the turn. Gear changing is allowed to get started from the stop.
- Maintain smooth speed. Make the turns smoothly without stops.
- Turn correctly. You must not turn too wide or short. Do not go over or touch the curb or cause other traffic to back up.

As you complete the turn the examiner will check to see if you:

- Check traffic.
- Are in the correct lane. You must finish the turn in the correct lane. For a left turn use the left lane and a right turn use the right lane.
- Cancel the signal. You must turn off the turn signal.
- For left turns accelerate and move right. You must accelerate smoothly and move into the right lane when traffic is clear.

When crossing railroad tracks the examiner will check that you:

- Check traffic. You should look left and right and roll down window to listen, and you may open door on buses.
- Do not change gears while on the tracks.
- Do not stop or brake on the tracks and do not make lane changes or pass on the tracks.
- Keep to posted speed limits.

The examiner may have you stop and start on a grade. When stopping on a grade the examiner will check that you:

- Check traffic prior to stopping.
- Turn signals on.
- Position the vehicle on the right side of the roadway.
- Slow down smoothly, changing gears to keep power and do not coast.

Once stopped the examiner will check that you:

- Have positioned the vehicle parallel to the curb.
- Do not let the vehicle roll forward or backward.
- Cancel the turn signal and turn on 4-way flashers.
- Put on the parking brake, put the gear shift in neutral, release the foot brake, and take foot off the clutch.

The examiner will tell you to continue and check that you:

- Check traffic.
- Turn 4-way flashers off and left turn signal on.
- Release the parking brake, put vehicle in gear, and do not turn the steering wheel before the vehicle moves.
- Do not stall engine when starting or roll backward.
- Continue to check traffic.
- Accelerate smoothly and blend with traffic.

As you drive up a grade, the examiner will check that you:

- Select the proper gear, change gears to maintain speed, and do not lug the engine.
- Stay in the rightmost lane.
- Keep hands on the steering wheel.
- Use 4-way flashers if too slow for traffic.
- Check traffic especially to the left and rear (use mirrors).

As you drive down a grade, the examiner will check that you:

- Select proper gear (lower gear) before the grade. Only gentle to moderate braking should be needed to control speed and engine RPMs.
- Do not ride the clutch.
- Check brakes by applying them before the grade.
- Maintain a steady speed and do not ride or fan the brakes.
- Stay in the rightmost lane and maintain correct following distance.
- Check traffic especially to the left and rear using your mirrors.

If you must stop at the intersection, the examiner will check the same items as when you stop for a turn.

As you drive through an intersection, the examiner will check that you:

- Check traffic.
- Yield to pedestrians and other traffic as required.
- Do not change lanes in the intersection.
- Do not change gears in the intersection.
- Do not lug or rev engine.
- Smoothly drive through the intersection without disrupting traffic.

As you drive down a straight city or county road, the examiner will check that you:

- Regularly check traffic, watch for hazards, and look far enough ahead (7 to 15 seconds).
- Select proper lane and stay to the center of the lane without wandering back and forth.
- Maintain correct speed and avoid continual slowing up, stopping, and accelerating.
- Maintain correct following distance. One second per 10 feet of vehicle length plus one additional second for speed over 40 MPH.

When you must change lanes, the examiner will check that you:

- Check traffic to front and rear especially the blind spot.
- Signal the lane change.
- Do not tailgate while waiting to change lanes.
- Make a smooth lane change and maintain your speed and allow correct distance between all vehicles.
- Cancel signal.

In curves, the examiner will check that you:

- Reduce your speed before the curve.
- Do not brake while in the curve.
- Maintain your speed during the curve without a strong pull to the side.
- Keep all vehicle wheels in your lane.
- Continually check traffic and use your mirrors to watch the tracking of your vehicle.

As you go under an underpass or over a bridge, the examiner may ask you:

- The posted height of the underpass.
- The weight limit of the bridge.

As you merge on the expressway, the examiner will check that you:

- Check traffic.
- Check the blind spot.
- Signal at least soon enough that expressway traffic can see the signal.
- Merge without stopping.
- Use acceleration lane to accelerate to traffic flow.
- Merge smoothly while maintaining following distance.
- Move to center of driving lane and cancel signal.

When changing lanes on the expressway, the examiner will check that you:

- Check traffic to front and rear expecially blind spots.
- Signal the lane change.
- Do not tailgate while waiting to change lanes.
- Make a smooth lane change, maintain your speed, and allow correct distance between all vehicles.
- Cancel signal.

As you exit the expressway, the examiner will check that you:

- Check traffic front and rear, especially to the right and in blind spots.
- Signal the exit.
- Smoothly enter the exit lane at the start of the exit lane.
- Slow down in the deceleration lane.
- Do not exceed the ramp speed and have no noticeable pull to the side on the ramp curve.
- Do not tailgate on the ramp.
- Cancel signal.

During the test the examiner will have you back up your vehicle. The examiner will check you as you back in a straight line and as you parallel park. Make sure you:

- Check your backing area.
- Sound your horn as a warning.
- Turn on 4-way flashers.
- Control your vehicle while backing.
- Do not run over curbs or course markings.
- Stop when directed by the examiner.

The examiner will have you forward stop your vehicle at a given point. Make sure you:

- Stop in one smooth braking action.

The examiner will check your general driving skills throughout the test. Make sure you:

- Use your clutch properly. Don't coast with clutch in, don't ride the clutch, don't snap the clutch, and don't lug or over rev the engine.
- Use gears correctly. Select correct gear and don't grind or clash gears.
- Use brakes correctly. Brake smoothly with steady pressure.
- Don't ride the brakes and don't brake hard or fan air brakes.
- Steer correctly, keep both hands on the wheel, and don't under or over control the steering.
- Obey all traffic signs and laws.
- Drive safely without an accident. Do not run over curbs or sidewalks. Stay in your traffic lane. Drive so you are never forced to take evasive action.
- Wear your seat belt.

Sample Evaluation Form

New York State Department of Motor Vehicles
COMMERCIAL DRIVER LICENSE — ROAD TEST EVALUATION

Validation Number	Current License Class:	Post:		Date of Test / /
Identification Number		License Class:	Temporary License Validation	
Applicant Name (Print as it appears on current license:)	Date of Birth / /	Endorsements:		
Applicant Signature ▶	Signature Check ☐ Yes ☐ No	Vehicle Restrictions:		
Examiner's Signature ▶	MVLE Number	Other Restrictions:		

I. PRE-TRIP INSPECTION	Q	DQ	U
A. Exterior Lights, Reflectors			
B. Tires, Rims, Lugs, Spacers, Seals			
C. Springs, Shocks			
D. Leaks			
E. Brakes			
F. Air/Electrical Lines			
G. Fifth Wheel			
H. Horn, Wipers, Heater, Defroster			
I. Gauges			
J. Safety Equipment (Fire Ext., etc.)			
K. Air Brakes Test			
L. 50 ft. Brake Test			
BUSES			
M. Emergency Exits			
N. Seats			
O. Passenger Entry			

II. BASIC SKILLS	Q	DQ	U
A. Parallel Park			
1. Observation			
2. Steering Control			
3. Pull-ups			
4. Too Far away from, or hit, curb			
B. Straight Line Backing			
1. Observation			
2. Steering Control			
3. Pull-ups			
C. Forward Stop			
1. Distance			
2. Brake Control			

III. ROAD HAZARD CHECKS	Q	DQ	U
A. Bridges			
B. Underpasses			
C. Railroad Crossing			
D. Other			

IV. TURNS & INTERSECTIONS	Q	DQ	U
A. Observation			
B. Steering Control			
C. Signaling			
D. Too Wide			
E. Too Short			
F. Proper Speed			
G. Engine Control			
H. Stopping Position			

V. GRADE CONTROL	Q	DQ	U
A. Observation			
B. Signaling			
C. Setting Controls			
D. Rolls on Grade			

VI. DRIVING UP/DOWN GRADE	Q	DQ	U
A. Proper Gear			
B. Proper Speed			
C. Observation			

VII. HIGHWAY DRIVING	Q	DQ	U
A. Observation			
B. Speed			
C. Entering			
D. Lane Changing			
E. Signaling			
F. Exiting			
G. Lane Position			

VIII. URBAN/RURAL DRIVING	Q	DQ	U
A. Observation			
B. Lane Position			
C. Signaling			
D. Lane Changes			
E. Speed			

IX. RIGHT AND LEFT CURVES	Q	DQ	U
A. Observation			
B. Stays in Lane			
C. Proper Speed			
D. Vehicle Control			

X. GENERAL DRIVING SKILLS	Q	DQ	U
A. Observation			
B. Steering Control			
C. Clutch Control			
D. Proper Use of Gears			
E. Proper Use of Brakes			
F. Obeys Traffic Signs and Signals			
G. Courtesy			

RESTRICTIONS & ENDORSEMENTS

R	☐	Tractor/Trailer (trailer greater than 10,000 lbs.)(A)
O	☐	Truck/Trailer (truck greater than 26,000 and trailer greater than 10,000) (A)
		OR
01	☐	Truck does not exceed 26,000
02	☐	Truck does not exceed 18,000
T	☐	Tractor Only (B)
M	☐	Bus — greater than 26,000 (B)
N	☐	Bus — less than 26,001 (C)
W	☐	Bus — less than 18,001 (C)
N1	☐	Bus — no vehicle designed Adult seating capacity of 15 or more
	☐	Truck greater than 26,000 (B)
	☐	Truck less than 26,001 (C)
	☐	Non-CDL C (18,001 - 26,000) (cannot have H or P Endorsement)
	☐	Farm Vehicle
	☐	A . . . . F Endorsement
	☐	B . . . . . . G Endorsement
	☐	Air Brakes (Yes)
L1	☐	No Air Brakes (A)
L2	☐	No Air Brakes (B)
L	☐	No Air Brakes Any Vehicle

☐ **QUALIFIED**

☐ **DISQUALIFIED FOR:**
   ☐ Accident
   ☐ Serious Violation
   ☐ Dangerous Action
   ☐ DQ in 4 or more categories
   ☐ Needs more experience

☐ **REDATE**

COMMENTS/REASON FOR REDATE
_____
_____
_____
_____
_____

CDL-200 (10/92)

PART THREE

*Study Material to Help
You Pass Your Tests*

DEALING WITH EMERGENCIES

Bus Operator

A bus operator is not a police officer, a firefighter, or an emergency services technician, nor is the bus operator expected to perform the duties of any of these. However, the bus operator is often in a position to spot emergencies before others know of them. The bus driver's seat is high above the street. This high perch gives the bus operator a good view of what is happening all around the area. Also, buses are out on the street at low-density hours and in weather conditions when few other people or vehicles are out. The bus operator might be the first to see smoke coming from a window, an automobile accident, or a victim of illness or violence lying in the gutter.

Bus operators also must handle emergencies which occur on their buses. Such emergencies might include injury from a fall upon entering or leaving the bus or in the aisle; sudden illness of a passenger; injury caused by one passenger to another; crime on the bus; and, worst of all scenarios, multiple injuries caused by an accident in which the bus is involved.

No bus operator is expected to single-handedly deal with such emergencies, but each does have some responsibility. The first responsibility of the bus operator who confronts an emergency on the bus or in the street is to summon competent help. If the bus is equipped with two-way communications, as most transit buses are, the operator must use these. If not, the operator may make generous use of the horn to attract the attention of police or bystanders who might send for help. The bus operator may not leave the bus if there are any passengers aboard. Therefore the services of a private citizen, passenger or pedestrian, must be enlisted to notify police, fire services, or emergency medical services of the location and the nature of the emergency.

Notification may be made by use of the nearest fire or police call box or public telephone.

The responsibility of the bus operator beyond summoning help is to safeguard the passengers. This means that the operator must use judgment in staying out of the line of fire of criminal activity in progress, in avoiding an area of dangerous road conditions, and in safely driving the bus out of problem areas and back to the route. The operator must take great care not to put his or her own life in danger because the safety of the passengers depends upon the skills and services of the bus operator.

Once professional assistance has been summoned, the bus operator should give first aid and emergency assistance to the extent to which he or she is capable. Some of the most common emergencies on the bus are likely to be the consequences of falls—bruises, broken bones, bleeding. Other health emergencies might stem from sudden illness—heart attack, asthma, diabetes—or from violence, such as stabbing.

The victim of a bus-related fall is seldom severely injured. Most can be seated and reassured that medical care is on the way. An elderly person who appears to be in great pain may indeed have broken a hip. This person should remain lying down and be kept warm until medics arrive. In any medical emergency, the bus should not proceed until help arrives. Most passengers will readily understand the delay. Passengers who object should be issued "blockage" transfers so that they may board another bus without additional fare.

Some other medical emergencies may require active first aid by the bus operator. Severe bleeding is very serious. An injured person may rapidly bleed to death if a major artery is severed. Therefore, along with sending for help, you must try to slow the bleeding. A person who is losing a lot of blood is likely to faint. So, have the person lie down. Raise the area of bleeding above the height of the heart if at all possible, cover the wound with a cloth (clean, if available), and apply firm, direct pressure. This may be unpleasant for you and painful for the victim, but you may be saving a life.

Heart attack, diabetic coma, asthma, and the like may require emergency assistance that can be given only by a fully trained and qualified person. If you are certified in CPR, you know when and how to administer it. If not, do not interfere. If you are very certain that your passenger has stopped breathing, then you should begin artificial respiration without delay.

Mouth-to-mouth resuscitation is today's most commonly used method of artificial respiration. It is simple enough to do without training or practice. Here are the steps:

1. Lay the victim on his or her back. Tilt the head back so that the chin points up. Clear the airway of any obstructions. Check to be certain that the person really is not breathing by watching for movement of the chest and by putting your ear against the mouth to listen for or feel exhaled breath.
2. If there are no signs of the victim's breathing,
    a) keep the victim's head tilted back and pinch the nose shut,
    b) take a deep breath,
    c) cover the victim's mouth tightly with your own open mouth and exhale into the victim's mouth. After exhaling two full breaths into the victim's mouth, remove your own mouth so that the victim can exhale.
    d) Watch for signs that victim is breathing independently. If the chest does not rise after the victim exhales, repeat the mouth-to-mouth breathing every 5 seconds (about 12 times a minute) until help arrives or until the victim begins breathing.
    e) If the victim is a child, cover both nose and mouth with your mouth and make more frequent, shallower breaths.

Fire on the bus is a very unlikely occurrence, and the most obvious action is to evacuate the bus at once. Passengers should be evacuated by the nearest safe route—exit doors and emergency exits at the end of the bus opposite that of the fire. Your biggest problem is keeping calm among the passengers and accomplishing an orderly departure. With the passengers off the bus, you may attempt to put out a small fire with your fire extinguisher. You should have a fire extinguisher or two on your bus, and your training period will have included instructions in use of the extinguishers. Know where the extinguishers are. Learn what type of extinguisher(s) you carry and the instructions for use before you ever need to use an extinguisher. Water can be used to put out wood, paper, or cloth fires or to cool a burning tire, but pouring water on most other fires can be dangerous. Water on a gasoline fire will just spread the flames. Water on an electrical fire creates a shock hazard. <u>If you have a fire extinguisher, it is safer to use it.</u> Use a B:C type of extinguisher on electrical fires and burning liquids. Use the A:B:C type for burning wood, paper, and cloth. Know what kind of extinguisher you have and know how it works. Study the instructions printed on the extinguisher before you set out in a new vehicle.

- Aim at the base of the fire, not into the flames.
- Stay as far from the fire as possible while using the extinguisher.
- Stand upwind of the fire. Let the wind blow the contents of the extinguisher into the fire, not the fire to the extinguisher.
- Use up the contents of the extinguisher even if you think that the fire is out. The fire could flare up again, and the extinguisher cannot be reused without recharging anyway.

A fire extinguisher may not be the best solution if a person is on fire. The best way to put out a fire on a person—whether it be the person's clothing or hair—is by smothering the fire. Wrap the person in blankets, coats, or a rug and roll the person over and over until the fire is out. Then keep the person lying down and loosely covered and send for medical help. Do not try to treat the burns yourself; do not try to make the person more comfortable by offering food or drink. Watch to make sure the person continues breathing and give words of comfort and reassurance if the person is conscious, but wait for a trained professional to give medical help.

Your bus operator exam may ask a few questions about dealing with emergencies or about first aid knowledge. Use your common sense and this information in choosing the best answer to these questions. The bus operator should remember not to step in where he or she is unqualified and may do more harm than good. However, if the greater harm would come from doing nothing, then the bus operator should do whatever he or she can to help.

Conductor

A conductor is also not a police officer, a firefighter, or an emergency services technician, and, like a bus operator, a conductor is not expected to perform the duties of the police officer, the firefighter, nor the emergency services technician. However, the conductor, by his or her position on the train, the platform, or elsewhere in the station or railroad yards, is often in a position to spot emergencies before others know of them. A conductor is likely to be the first to see a medical emergency such as a victim of illness, accident, or violence or a potential emergency such as excessive debris on the tracks, a small fire, or suspicious activity. In every instance, it is the responsibility of the conductor to safeguard the lives of patrons and employees of the transit system.

Most often, the first response to an emergency is to summon competent help. If the emergency occurs at a station, this is no problem. Subway stations are patrolled by transit police officers who are equipped to call for medical or firefighting help, for police reinforcements, and for expert technical mechanical assistance. If no transit police officer is in sight, then the conductor should notify the station master, station supervisor, or another transit employee nearby. Token clerks are equipped with telephones. If the conductor cannot leave the scene of the emergency, he or she might send word to the token clerk with a bystander.

An emergency on a moving train can pose more difficulty in terms of notification. If there is a transit police officer on board, the officer may be in a distant car. The train operator is, of course, in the front cab, and other conductors are not in your car keeping you company. This is the time to use portable communications equipment—walkie-talkie or telephone if available—or, if you have the time and maneuverability, to rush into another car. You may have to communicate with other transit personnel over the train's public address system. Use of the emergency brake cord is a last resort. Once the emergency cord has been pulled, startup is a drawn-out, laborious procedure. If the emergency is an illness or injury, it is more important to keep the train moving and to get to the next station for help. If the emergency would be worsened by continued motion of the train—a person has fallen between the cars—then the emergency stop is the right course of action. A conductor who faces an emergency on a moving train may well have to deal with that emergency on his or her own.

Emergencies in the yards or at terminal points may be very dangerous and severe, but the conductor seldom is alone at these locations. There are nearly always co-workers to sound the alarm and to help with the immediate situation as well.

Subway trains are operated by electricity. The electricity is carried in the third rail. Contact with the high voltage of the third rail is almost certain to lead to death. All subway personnel are trained to avoid contact with the third rail and are instructed in means of shutting off the power. But, shutting off the power disrupts a whole line. Far better is to avoid the necessity of shutting it off. The conductor must be alert to overcrowding and pushing and shoving on platforms that might lead to an accidental fall. The alert conductor notices suspicious-looking characters who might deliberately push someone or who might jump. The conductor must also be aware of a passenger who appears to be ill or intoxicated or otherwise out of control and who might fall onto the tracks. The conductor must be ready to step between the platform edge and people and to control people's actions.

No matter how careful and well-trained the worker, accidents can happen. A worker can slip and lose his or her footing or can be knocked over by a swinging object. No matter how watchful a platform conductor, a passenger may fall to the tracks. The power MUST be cut off before the person can be touched. The human body conducts electricity. This means that the rescuer who touches a victim still in contact with live electricity will have the electricity transmitted to him or herself. Never touch an electric shock victim until he or she has been fully separated from the electric source. If the cause of the electric shock is a loose live wire rather than the third rail, the victim may survive. If the source of the power is unknown, the person must be pushed away from the wire with a nonmetallic instrument such as a board, a rubber tire, or heavy rope.

A victim of electric shock may have burns and may have stopped breathing. Burns should be covered loosely with clean cloths; nothing more. Breathing stoppage requires artificial respiration.

Mouth-to-mouth resuscitation is today's most commonly used method of artificial respiration. It is simple enough to do without training or practice. Here are the steps:

1. Lay the victim on his or her back. Tilt the head back so that the chin points up. Clear the airway of any obstructions. Check to be certain that the person really is not breathing by watching for movement of the chest and by putting your ear against the mouth to listen for or feel exhaled breath.
2. If there are no signs of the victim's breathing,
    a) keep the victim's head tilted back and pinch the nose shut,
    b) take a deep breath,
    c) cover the victim's mouth tightly with your own open mouth and exhale into the victim's mouth. After exhaling two full breaths into the victim's mouth, remove your own mouth so that the victim can exhale.
    d) Watch for signs that the victim is breathing independently. If the chest does not rise after the victim exhales, repeat the mouth-to-mouth breathing every 5 seconds (about 12 times a minute) until help arrives or until the victim begins breathing.
    e) If the victim is a child, cover both nose and mouth with your mouth and make more frequent, shallower breaths.

Electric shock is not a hazard on moving trains, but passengers may become ill on the trains. Most illnesses can wait for medics who will meet the train at the next station. The job of the conductor is to somehow alert medics of the problem. If portable radio is available, the call for help may be made from a moving train. If the conductor has no means for communicating with the street-bound world and feels he or she should stay in the car with the ill passenger, then the conductor must use the public address system to communicate with the motorman to request a stop and phone call at the next station.

Some illnesses respond best to immediate first aid. A conductor who is certified in CPR may resuscitate a heart attack victim, but a conductor not so certified should not make the attempt. However, if a passenger is not breathing, the conductor is obliged to immediately begin artificial respiration as described above. Artificial respiration does not require special training or certification and is a known life saver.

Fire and smoke present unique problems underground. On moving or stopped trains, smoke is the more likely problem. Part of a conductor's training includes extensive instruction in evacuation of subway trains. The conductor must determine the quickest

safe route by which to move passengers away from the source of the smoke. The conductor must first use judgment regarding direction in which to lead passengers and whether to hold them in a far car or evacuate the entire train. If evacuation is called for, the conductor must be certain power is off and it is safe to proceed. Then the conductor must use tact and people skills in explaining the problem without alarming the passengers and producing panic.

Smoke is, of course, produced by fire. If the conductor is on an operating train, the fire is the problem of other personnel. However, the conductor may notice a track fire on an adjoining track or in the yards during switching or in a station during a stop or even while walking across a platform. At the very first sign of a fire—on the tracks, in a station, or in the yards—summon the fire department. A fire can get out of hand very quickly, and the sooner the fire department is alerted the better, even if the fire can be managed by transit employees. In a station, notify all available personnel to evacuate passengers from the area. Then, if the fire is still small, try to put it out. Know the locations of fire extinguishers in the station and on the trains. Learn what type of extinguisher(s) you carry and the instructions for use before you ever need to use an extinguisher. Water can be used to put out wood, paper, or cloth fires or to cool a burning tire, but pouring water on most other fires can be dangerous. Water on a gasoline fire will just spread the flames. Water on an electrical fire creates a shock hazard. If you have a fire extinguisher, it is safer to use it. Use a B:C type of extinguisher on electrical fires and burning liquids. Use the A:B:C type for burning wood, paper, and cloth. Know what kind of extinguisher you have and know how it works. Study the instructions printed on the extinguisher before you set out in a new vehicle.

- Aim at the base of the fire, not into the flames.
- Stay as far from the fire as possible while using the extinguisher.
- Stand upwind of the fire. Let the wind blow the contents of the extinguisher into the fire, not the fire to the extinguisher.
- Use up the contents of the extinguisher even if you think that the fire is out. The fire could flare up again, and the extinguisher cannot be reused without recharging anyway.

A fire extinguisher may not be the best solution if a person is on fire. The best way to put out a fire on a person—whether it be the person's clothing or hair—is by smothering the fire. Wrap the person in blankets, coats, or a rug and roll the person over and over until the fire is out. Then keep the person lying down and loosely covered and send for medical help. Do not try to treat the burns yourself; do not try to make the person more comfortable by offering food or drink. Watch to make sure the person continues breathing and give words of comfort and reassurance if the person is conscious, but wait for a trained professional to give medical help.

Subway station and trackyard accidents are most likely to involve falls. Slip and fall accidents on platforms, steps, and along the rails may involve simple bruises and general shaking up of the victim or may result in broken bones. You can use a little common sense when dealing with broken bones. A person with a broken arm or hand can walk out of harm's way and wait for transportation to medical services. A person who may have broken bones in a foot in a fall or by dropping a heavy object can hop from a heavy traffic area and be seated on a bench or railroad tie to await help. On the other hand, the victim who has fallen down a full flight of stairs or from the platform onto the trackbed or from a height in the yard and is lying still should not be moved. Whenever the head, neck, or back may have been injured, there is the real danger of spinal cord injury. A severe spinal cord injury can leave the victim crippled for life. Only a trained person should move the victim if there is any possibility at all of a spinal cord injury. If a coworker or a passenger is hurt in this way, the best assistance you can give is to create a safe island in which the person lies awaiting the emergency medical services crew. This means turning off power so that no moving train can enter the area to hit the person on the track. On a platform it means directing pedestrian traffic wide around the injured person. If the victim has fallen to the bottom of the stairs, cordoning off the entire staircase might be the wisest move. Cover the victim lightly and await the paramedics who have equipment to move the victim without causing further injury.

The injuries associated with falls do not usually lead to heavy bleeding. Injuries caused by swinging objects or falls against pointed or sharp edged objects in the yards, however, can lead to nasty cuts or puncture wounds. Another source of wounds with serious bleeding is violence. There is some amount of crime everywhere, and the subways are not immune. Sometimes violence among members of a group spills into the subway while in progress. Sometimes the violence occurs while a person is committing a crime, generally robbery at gunpoint or knifepoint. Crime is the conductor's nightmare. The conductor must safeguard other passengers, notify other transit personnel and the authorities, and assist the victim.

Severe bleeding may require active assistance. An injured person may rapidly bleed to death if a major artery is severed. Therefore, along with sending for help, you must try to slow the bleeding. A person who is losing a lot of blood is likely to faint. So, have the person lie down. Raise the area of bleeding above the height of the heart if at all possible, cover the wound with a cloth (clean, if available), and apply firm, direct pressure. This may be unpleasant for you and painful for the victim, but you may be saving a life.

Your conductor exam may ask a few questions about dealing with emergencies or about first aid knowledge. Use your common sense and this information in choosing the best answer to these questions. The conductor should remember not to step in where he or she is unqualified and may do more harm than good. However, if the greater harm would come from doing nothing, then the conductor should do whatever he or she can to help.

VEHICLE SAFETY

The bus operator is not expected to be a trained mechanic; however, he or she is expected to be aware of the condition of the vehicle and to take responsibility for reporting problems or dangerous conditions.

In some localities, the same driver operates the same vehicle every day. This driver gets to know the vehicle well and can quickly recognize when it doesn't handle, sound, feel, or smell just right. The driver who takes out the same vehicle each day may be personally responsible for minor adjustments and even for routine care. Daily reporting may not be required. This driver may just bring the vehicle for regularly scheduled maintenance and when there is a problem.

In most localities, and certainly in big cities, drivers are assigned to vehicles on a daily basis. A careful morning checkout of the vehicle is more important to the driver who is using an unfamiliar vehicle. If a driver does not know the special "feel" of a particular vehicle, he or she must be even more careful to check for potential problems. Likewise, the driver who turns in a vehicle in the evening that someone else may drive the next day has the extra responsibility of filing a complete and accurate report on its condition. That driver must make a turn-in inspection and fill out whatever reports are required.

Check-out and check-in inspections make sense in terms of personal safety of drivers and passengers and in terms of maintaining the life of department vehicles. Daily safety inspections are required by law.

You will be required to do daily safety inspections by your department, and you will have to learn to do these to pass the Class B Commercial Driver's License Test (CDL). There are far more drivers of tractor trailers, tank trucks, double trailers, and other heavy-duty, long-distance haulers than there are drivers of transit buses. The CDL was drafted to apply to all of them. Daily inspections are even more necessary and more meaningful when the vehicle may have covered 600 miles that day. But, since you have to take the same test that those drivers have to take, you may as well learn what you can about daily vehicle inspection.

The first thing to do at the beginning of the day when assigned your bus is to look at the previous driver's defect card. Have all the reported problems been corrected? If not, do not proceed without direction from your supervisor. If the reported defects have direct bearing on safety, the bus should not go into service. If yesterday's problems are no longer problems, you can begin your own inspection. If your department has a prescribed order for inspection, follow it. If not, you can follow our suggested order to create a routine that works best for you. Just be sure to do your inspection the same way every day so that you are certain not to miss any important points.

The first part of your inspection is done without touching the vehicle at all. Basically, you look. Look under the vehicle. Is there a puddle? Use your eyes and your nose. A gasoline leak will be close to the gasoline tank and will smell distinctly like gasoline. Antifreeze/coolant is green. Motor oil is brown and is thick and greasy. Transmission fluid is also oily but is pinkish and is a thinner oil.

After looking for puddles, look at wheels and tires. Be sure all tires are properly inflated. Mechanics should be monitoring tread depth for you, but you can double check. Also look at the tire sidewalls. Steel cords or fabric popping out at the sidewalls is very dangerous. You should not drive at all on tires with worn or damaged sidewalls. Be sure all lugs are in place and tight and that rims are not bent or damaged. And take a look at valve stems to be sure that they are in good condition. If even one tire leaks air while you are on the road, you will find maneuvering more difficult.

Don't crawl under the vehicle, but take a look at the tail pipe and other visible parts of the exhaust system to be sure that the pipe is not missing, broken, or compressed.

As you walk around the vehicle checking for leaks and tire condition, notice the lights. If the glass is dirty, wash the headlamps, taillights, signals, flashers, reflectors, etc. You need to have clean lights in order to see and to be seen. This is such a simple safety measure, yet it really pays off.

As long as you are wiping or washing off the lights, hop up and do the same for mirrors and windshield. As you can see, much of the daily inspection is really based on common sense. Obviously, greater visibility leads to greater safety. While looking at the windshield, check the wiper blades to be certain that they are secure and that they make contact with the windows throughout their length.

As you walk around the vehicle, you may notice body damage or hairline cracks or tiny holes in windshield or other glass. Mark these down. You don't want it on your record that you damaged a vehicle that you found already damaged. And tiny breaks or holes in the windshield can be repaired before they become so large that the whole piece of glass needs to be replaced. Bring small problems to the attention of the supervisor or mechanics so that they can be attended to at the next regularly scheduled overhaul or even sooner if necessary. While walking around the bus, check for dangling wires, tools, or debris on the ground or garage floor that might be in your way when you back up or pull out. Be sure you have a clear, safe path.

Now get into the driver's seat. Try the horn. Turn on lights one-by-one and make certain that all of them work. You may need someone to stand behind the vehicle to tell you whether your brake lights and backup lights are working properly. Turn on the windshield wipers and try the washers. Everything should work. Start the engine and listen for strange noises. Look at all the gages and warning lights. Some of these may not be operative until the engine has been running for awhile or until the vehicle is in motion, but watch all those that might indicate problems in a stationary vehicle. With the engine running, you can test the brakes for pressure even if not for stopping speed or balance. You should also check the steering wheel to be sure it does not have too much play. You want the steering wheel to be responsive when you turn it.

Before you get out of the vehicle, check to be certain that your two-way radio, fire extinguishers, safety triangles or flares, extra fuses, and any other required safety devices are in place. Look into the first aid kit and make sure all supplies are in place. If any items in the first aid kit have been used, resupply before starting out. Finally, open and shut all doors. Make sure that they latch securely.

The next place to look is under the hood or in the engine compartment. There are many safety checks you can make here without any formal mechanical training. First, check fluid levels. The fluid levels you can easily check are:

- Motor oil
- Transmission fluid
- Brake fluid
- Power steering fluid

- Radiator coolant
- Windshield washer fluid
- Battery level

Next look at belts and hoses. Belts and hoses must be securely attached and must be neither stiff and rigid nor soft and spongy. There must be no nicks or cuts which could lead to breakage on the road. If you are not certain as to just how belts and hoses should feel, ask a supervisor. There is a very distinct feel to dried-out rubber and to rotting rubber. Once you have been shown, you will know how firm but flexible belts and hoses feel.

Also in the engine compartment you should look out for loose electrical connections, frayed wires, or buildup of deposits of any sort. If you notice any wires or parts that seem wobbly or out of line, ask for a second opinion. You are not expected to be an expert; you are expected to be alert to potential problems or safety hazards.

Your responsibility for vehicle safety does not end when you leave the garage. While driving, you must keep your eyes open for irregularities on any of the gages. Listen for unusual sounds. Notice if the steering is not responsive, if shifting is difficult, if acceleration is not as expected, if brakes grab unevenly, or if there is excessive pull. Stop on a hill and check to be sure that the emergency brake holds the vehicle securely. While driving and when you stop, use your nose—gasoline leaks announce themselves by their smell. Burning rubber, also, has a strong, distinctive smell. Burning rubber may come from double tires that are touching, from a belt that is travelling badly, from faulty transmission, or from brake problems. Bring the vehicle back in for service if you smell burning rubber. Carbon monoxide, the most dangerous component of exhaust has no smell; however, gasoline exhaust fumes do have an odor. If you smell exhaust inside your moving vehicle, you must suspect a problem with the exhaust system. If this is the case, you are breathing in carbon monoxide along with the other exhaust fumes. The exhaust system of this vehicle must be checked out and repaired very soon.

As the operator of a passenger bus, you must also be concerned with passenger safety items. Are all seats bolted to the floor? Are doors secure? What about emergency exit handles and regular-use railings and handholds. Do the signaling devices work properly? Once underway, you must watch that the aisles are kept clear of objects that passengers might trip over. And, in wet or icy weather, you must keep alert to slippery steps and aisles. Warn the passengers often if it is slippery underfoot.

In short, vehicle safety is a full-time concern—for your departmental written exam, for the CDL exam, when you start out each day, and throughout the working day as well.

MUNICIPAL GEOGRAPHY

Bus operators and subway conductors must be thoroughly familiar with the city so that they can consult transit maps with ease and direct passengers. Your exam will not ask you to know which subway lines and bus routes to take to a particular destination, but you will be expected to know where major points of interest are located. You must also know how to use transit maps.

The lists that follow include many of the most asked for locations in the city. You are surely familiar with many of these already. Learn as many more as you can. A good knowledge of the city will help you score high on the exam and will help you on the job.

Manhattan Neighborhoods

Chelsea: On the west side south of 31st Street, west of Sixth Avenue, north of 14th Street, and east of the Hudson River. Home of the flower market.

Chinatown: Downtown south of Canal Street and east and west of Bowery. Centered particularly along Bayard, Pell, and Mott Streets east of Bowery.

East Village: A downtown area south of 14th Street and north of East Houston Street, east of Broadway and west of First Avenue over to Avenues A, B, and C. Once the home of hippies and flower children, now home to many artists.

Financial District: Also known as Lower Manhattan, it is south of Vesey and Ann Streets, west of the East River, north of Water Street and Battery Park, and east of the Hudson River. This is the oldest part of the city and its financial hub.

Garment and Fur District: Midtown south of 42nd Street and north of 30th Street, west of Sixth and east of Eighth Avenues. The fashion capital of the United States.

Greenwich Village: A downtown area bounded on the north by 14th Street, on the east by Broadway, on the south by West Houston Street, and on the west by Greenwich Avenue. New York's bohemian neighborhood.

Harlem: Uptown north of 110th Street and south of 165th Street, east of Morningside Avenue and St. Nicholas Avenue, and west of the Harlem River.

Little Italy: Downtown south of Houston Street, west of Chrystie Street, north of Canal Street, and east of Broadway. Its heart is Mulberry Street.

Lower East Side: Also south of Houston Street but east of Little Italy and north of Chinatown. Grand and Orchard Streets are known for bargain shopping.

Midtown: As its name implies, the effective middle (though not its geographic center) of Manhattan. Midtown extends from the East River to the Hudson River between 59th Street and 14th Street.

Murray Hill and Gramercy Park: Midtown from Fifth Avenue east to First

Avenue and from 42nd Street south to 14th Street. This is an area housing some of the finest old residences mixed with commercial development.

SoHo: This neighborhood is just west of Little Italy and gets its name by lying south of Houston. It is west of Broadway, north of Canal Street, and east of the Avenue of the Americas. The heart of this artist's colony is West Broadway, Spring Street, and Greene Street.

Spanish Harlem: Directly east of Harlem starting at East 96th Street.

Theater District or Times Square area: Midtown south of 53rd Street, west of Avenue of the Americas, north of 40th Street, and east of Eighth Avenue. Its focal point is the intersection of Broadway and Seventh Avenue.

Tribeca: South of Canal Street, west of Broadway, north of Chambers Street, and east of the Hudson River. The artists' colony of SoHo just to the north has spilled into this neighborhood.

Upper East Side: Basically Manhattan from Central Park to the East River, that is, 59th Street to 110th Street.

Upper West Side: Again, Central Park to the Hudson River.

Washington Heights: The northern tip of Manhattan Island.

Sports and Recreation Facilities

Aqueduct Race Track: In Queens near Cross Bay Boulevard just off Belt Parkway.

Belmont Park Race Track: Close-in Long Island—Hempstead Turnpike, Cross Island Parkway, and Plainfield Avenue.

Flushing Meadow-Corona Park: In Queens on Grand Central Parkway.

Madison Square Garden: In Manhattan between Seventh and Eighth Avenues and West 31st and 33rd Streets.

Meadowlands Stadium and Byrne Arena: East Rutherford, NJ.

Nassau Veterans Memorial Coliseum: Hempstead, LI.

Riis Beach: Rockaway, Queens.

Rockefeller Center Skating Rink: Between Fifth and Sixth Avenues and 48th to 50th Streets, Manhattan

Shea Stadium: Flushing, Queens.

Wollman Skating Rink: In Central Park, Manhattan. Enter at 59th Street near Fifth Avenue.

Yankee Stadium: In the Bronx at 161st Street and River Avenue.

Yonkers Raceway: In Yonkers, Westchester County, just over the line from the Bronx at Yonkers and Central Avenues.

Concert Halls

Brooklyn Academy of Music: In Brooklyn at 30 Lafayette Avenue.

Brooklyn Center for the Performing Arts: At Brooklyn College, Nostrand Avenue and Avenue H.

Carnegie Hall: Seventh Avenue & 57th Street, Manhattan.

Lincoln Center for the Performing Arts: In Manhattan at 140 West 65th Street. The complex includes **Metropolitan Opera House**; **Avery Fisher Hall**; **Alice Tully Hall**; **Juilliard School of Music**; **New York State Theater**; **Vivian Beaumont Theater**; and **Mitzi Newhouse Theater**.

Tisch Center for the Performing Arts: 92nd Street Y, 92nd Street at Lexington Avenue, Manhattan.

Town Hall: In Manhattan at 113 West 43rd Street.

Museums

American Craft Museum: 40 West 53rd Street, Manhattan.

American Museum and Hayden Planetarium: Central Park West and 83rd Street, Manhattan.

American Museum of Immigration: Base of the Statue of Liberty.

American Museum of the Moving Image: 35th Avenue at 36th Street, Astoria, Queens.

American Museum of Natural History: Central Park West at 79th Street, Manhattan.

Asia Society Galleries: 725 Park Avenue at 70th Street, Manhattan.

Bible House: American Bible Society, 1865 Broadway at 61st Street, Manhattan.

Bronx Museum of the Arts: 1040 Grand Concourse, Bronx.

Brooklyn Museum: 200 Eastern Parkway at Washington Avenue, Brooklyn.

Brooklyn Children's Museum: 145 Brooklyn Avenue, Brooklyn.

Brooklyn's History Museum: The Brooklyn Historical Society, 128 Pierrepont Street, Brooklyn.

The Cloisters: Fort Tryon Park off Henry Hudson Parkway, top of Manhattan.

Cooper-Hewitt Museum: 2 East 91st Street, Manhattan.

Ellis Island Immigration Museum: Ellis Island, ferry from the Battery in Manhattan.

El Museo del Barrio: 1230 Fifth Avenue, Manhattan.

Fraunces Tavern Museum: 54 Pearl Street, Manhattan.

The Frick Collection: 1 East 70th Street at Fifth Avenue, Manhattan.

Hispanic Society of America: Broadway between West 155th and 156th Streets, Manhattan.

International Center of Photography: 1133 Avenue of the Americas at 43rd Street, Manhattan.

The Intrepid Sea-Air-Space Museum: Pier 68, Hudson River at foot of West 46th Street, Manhattan.

Jacques Marchais Center of Tibetan Art: 338 Lighthouse Avenue between New Dorp and Richmondtown, Staten Island.

Jewish Museum: 1109 Fifth Avenue at East 92nd Street, Manhattan.

Metropolitan Museum of Art, Fifth Avenue at 82nd Street, Manhattan.

Museum of American Folk Art: 2 Lincoln Square, Columbus Avenue between 65th and 66th Streets, Manhattan.

Museum of the American Indian: Broadway and West 155th Street, Manhattan.

Museum of Broadcasting: 1 East 53rd Street, Manhattan.

Museum of Bronx History: 3266 Bainbridge Avenue at East 208th Street, Bronx.

Museum of the City of New York: 1220 Fifth Avenue between 103rd and 104th Streets, Manhattan.

Museum of Holography: 11 Mercer Street, Manhattan.

Museum of Modern Art: 11 West 53rd Street, Manhattan.

New York Historical Society: 170 Central Park West, Manhattan.

New York Public Library: Fifth Avenue between 40th and 42nd Streets, Manhattan.

New York Public Library at Lincoln Center—Library and Museum of the Performing Arts: Broadway at 65th Street, Manhattan.

New York Transit Museum: Boerum Place and Schermerhorn Street, Brooklyn.

Pierpont Morgan Library: 29 East 36th Street, Manhattan.

Police Museum: 235 East 20th Street, Manhattan.

Queens Museum: NYC Building, Flushing Meadows-Corona Park, Queens.

Solomon R. Guggenheim Museum: 1071 Fifth Avenue, Manhattan.

South Street Seaport Museum: 207 Front Street, Manhattan.

Staten Island Children's Museum: 1000 Richmond Terrace at Snug Harbor, Staten Island.

Studio Museum in Harlem: 144 West 125th Street, Manhattan.

Whitney Museum of American Art: 945 Madison Avenue, Manhattan.

Parks and Squares

Battery Park: Foot of Broadway, Manhattan.

Bronx Park: Both sides of Bronx River, Bronx.

Central Park: West 59th Street to West 110th Street, Fifth Avenue to Central Park West, Manhattan.

City Hall Park: Broadway at Park Row.

Columbus Circle: 59th Street at Seventh Avenue, Broadway, and Eighth Avenue, Manhattan.

Fort Tryon Park: Washington Heights, Manhattan.

Herald Square: Broadway and Sixth Avenue at West 34th Street, Manhattan.

Jacob Riis Park: Far Rockaway, Queens.

Madison Square: From Fifth Avenue to Madison Avenue between 23rd and 26th Streets, Manhattan.

Morningside Park: From West 110th Street to West 123rd Street, Manhattan.

Mount Morris Park: Madison Avenue at 120th Street, Manhattan.

Pelham Bay Park: East Bronx along Eastchester and Pelham Bays.

Prospect Park: East-central Brooklyn.

Riverside Park: Along the Hudson River from 72nd Street to West 157th Street, Manhattan.

Sheridan Square: Greenwich Village, Manhattan.

Union Square: Broadway between 14th and 18th Streets, Manhattan.

Van Cortlandt Park: West Bronx north of 240th Street to City Line, Bronx

Washington Square: At southern end of Fifth Avenue, Manhattan.

Bridges and Tunnels

Brooklyn Battery Tunnel: Battery in Manhattan to Red Hook, Brooklyn.

Brooklyn Bridge: City Hall, Manhattan to downtown Brooklyn.

Cross Bay Parkway Bridge: Across Jamaica Bay from Howard Beach to the Rockaways, Queens.

George Washington Bridge: 179th Street, Manhattan to Fort Lee, NJ.

Henry Hudson Bridge: Over the Spuyten Duyvil where the Hudson River joins the Harlem, connecting the Bronx with Manhattan.

Holland Tunnel: Chambers Street in lower Manhattan to New Jersey.

Lincoln Tunnel: 38th Street, Manhattan to Weehawken, NJ.

Manhattan Bridge: Canal Street, Manhattan to downtown Brooklyn.

Midtown Tunnel: East 40th Street, Manhattan to Long Island City, Queens.

Queensborough Bridge: 59th Street, Manhattan to Long Island City, Queens.

Third Avenue Bridge: 127th Street, Manhattan to 134th Street, Bronx.

Throgs Neck Bridge: Locust Point, East Bronx to Whitestone, Queens.

Triboro Bridge: Connects 125th Street, Manhattan, Port Morris, Bronx, and Astoria, Queens.

Verrazano Narrows Bridge: Ft. Hamilton, Bay Ridge, Brooklyn to Ft. Wadsworth, South Beach, Staten Island.

Whitestone Bridge: Ferry Point Park, Bronx to Whitestone, Queens.

Williamsburg Bridge: Delancey Street on the lower east side of Manhattan to Broadway in Williamsburg, Brooklyn.

Willis Avenue Bridge: 125th Street, Manhattan to the South Bronx.

Other Major Points of Interest

American Stock Exchange: 86 Trinity Place, Manhattan.

Bartow-Pell Mansion: Shore Road in Pelham Bay Park, Bronx.

Bowling Green: Battery Park, Manhattan.

Bowne House: 37-01 Bowne Street, Flushing, Queens.

Bronx Wildlife Conservation Park, formerly **Bronx Zoo**: In Bronx Park south of Fordham Road and Bronx River Parkway, Bronx.

Brooklyn Botanic Garden: Along Eastern Parkway and Washington and Flatbush Avenues, Brooklyn.

Castle Clinton National Monument: Battery Park, Manhattan.

Cathedral Church of St. John the Divine: Amsterdam Avenue and 112th Street, Manhattan.

Chrysler Building: Lexington Avenue at 42nd Street, Manhattan.

The Church of the Ascension: 10th Street and Fifth Avenue, Manhattan.

City Hall: Broadway between Chambers and Barclay Streets, Manhattan.

City Island: In Pelham Bay, Bronx. Reached by causeways.

Citicorp Center: 53rd Street and Lexington Avenue, Manhattan.

Columbia University: Broadway and 116th Street, Manhattan.

Coney Island: Surf Avenue, Ocean Parkway and 37th Street, Brooklyn.

Conference House: 7455 Hylan Boulevard, Tottenville, Staten Island.

Cooper Union: Between Third and Fourth Avenues at Seventh Street, Manhattan.

Discount Ticket Locations:
Manhattan TKTS—Broadway & 47th Street.
Manhattan TKTS—2 World Trade Center.
Music & Dance Booth—Bryant Park, 42nd Street east of 6th Avenue, Manhattan.
Brooklyn—in front of Boro Hall at Court and Montague Streets.

Dyckman House Park and Museum: 4881 Broadway at 204th Street, Manhattan.

Ellis Island: In New York Harbor. Ferry from Battery Park, Manhattan or Liberty Park, New Jersey.

Empire State Building: 350 Fifth Avenue at 34th Street, Manhattan.

Federal Hall National Memorial: 26 Wall Street, Manhattan.

Federal Reserve Bank of New York: 33 Liberty Street, Manhattan.

Flatiron Building: Fifth Avenue at 23rd Street, Manhattan.

Fulton Fish Market: Fulton and South Streets, Manhattan.

Grand Central Terminal: 42nd Street and Park Avenue, Manhattan.

Grant's Tomb: Riverside Drive and West 122nd Street, Manhattan.

Guiness World of Records: In the Empire State Building.

Hall of Fame for Great Americans: West 181st Street and University Avenue, Bronx.

Hayden Planetarium: 81st Street and Central Park West, Manhattan.

Jacob K. Javits Convention Center: 34th to 39th Streets between Eleventh and Twelfth Avenues, Manhattan.

John F. Kennedy Airport: Southeast Queens edge of Jamaica Bay.

LaGuardia Airport: Off Grand Central Parkway, East Elmhurst, Queens.

Little Church Around the Corner: Fifth Avenue and 29th Street, Manhattan.

Macy's: On Herald Square, 34th Street and Broadway, Manhattan.

Morris-Jumel Mansion: West 160th Street and Edgecombe Avenue, Manhattan.

New York Aquarium for Wildlife Conservation: Boardwalk and West Eighth Street, Coney Island, Brooklyn.

New York Botanical Garden: In Bronx Park, Southern Boulevard entrance, Bronx.

New York Public Library: Fifth Avenue and 42nd Street, Manhattan.

New York Stock Exchange: 20 Broad Street, Manhattan.

New York University: On and near Washington Square, Manhattan.

One Times Square: 42nd Street and Broadway, Manhattan.

Pennsylvania Station: Seventh Avenue between West 31st and 33rd Streets, Manhattan.

Plymouth Church of the Pilgrims: Orange Street between Hicks and Henry Streets, Brooklyn.

Poe Cottage: Grand Concourse and East Kingsbridge Road, Bronx.

Post Office (main): 31st to 33rd Streets on Eighth Avenue, Manhattan.

Queens Botanical Garden: 43-50 Main Street, Queens.

Radio City Music Hall: Rockefeller Center, 50th Street and Avenue of the Americas, Manhattan.

Richmondtown Restoration: 441 Clarke Avenue and Arthur Kill Road, Richmond, Staten Island.

Riverside Church: 490 Riverside Drive at 120th Street, Manhattan.

Rockefeller Center: Fifth to Sixth Avenues, 47th to 51st Streets, Manhattan.

Roosevelt Island Tramway: 59th Street at the East River, Manhattan.

Schomburg Center for Research in Black Culture: 515 Lenox Avenue at West 135th Street, Manhattan.

South Street Seaport: Along the East River south of the Brooklyn Bridge, Manhattan.

Snug Harbor Cultural Center: 1000 Richmond Terrace, Staten Island.

St. Mark's-in-the-Bowery: Second Avenue and 10th Street, Manhattan.

St. Patrick's Cathedral: Fifth Avenue and 50th Street, Manhattan.

St. Paul's Chapel: Fulton Street and Broadway, Manhattan.

Staten Island Ferry: South Ferry at foot of Manhattan to St. George, Staten Island.

Staten Island Zoo: In Barrett Park between Broadway and Clove Road, West New Brighton, Staten Island.

Statue of Liberty: On Liberty Island (Bedloe's Island) in New York Harbor. Ferry from Battery Park or Liberty State Park, NJ.

Temple Emanu-El: Fifth Avenue and 65th Street, Manhattan.

Theater District: Sixth to Ninth Avenues, 41st to 53rd Streets, Manhattan.

Theodore Roosevelt Birthplace National Historic Site: 28 East 20th Street, Manhattan.

Trinity Church: Broadway and Wall Street, Manhattan.

Trump Tower: 56th Street and Fifth Avenue, Manhattan.

United Nations: First Avenue from 42nd to 48th Streets, Manhattan.

US Custom House: South side of Bowling Green, Battery Park, Manhattan.

Van Cortlandt Mansion: Van Cortlandt Park, North of Broadway at 246th Street, Bronx.

Wall Street: Downtown, east from Broadway, Manhattan.

Wave Hill: 675 West 252nd Street, Riverdale, Bronx.

Woolworth Building: 233 Broadway, Manhattan.

World Trade Center: Downtown off Church Street, Manhattan.